NATIONAL INCOME AND EXPENDITURE

by

RICHARD

AND

GIOVANNA

STONE

BOWES AND BOWES
LONDON

CONTENTS

CONTENTS

INTRODUCTION

NATIONAL INCOME is a household phrase and in a general way what it means is obvious: it is the income of a nation as opposed to the income of an individual. But like many phrases in common use it may not have quite the same meaning to all who use it. If we probe more deeply and ask how it is defined we shall have to clarify many concepts which are fundamental to the study of economics and to the conduct of business affairs. If we go further and ask how it is measured we shall find ourselves surveying almost the whole field of economic statistics. When we reach the end we shall have outlined the anatomy of an economic system and obtained both a clear picture of the circular flow of economic activity and an essential tool for understanding many of the central problems of economic life.

Coming down to brass tacks, let us equip ourselves with a copy of the official Blue Book on *National Income and Expenditure* [34] which comes out each year in September. From small beginnings in the form of a White Paper issued with the Budget of 1941, this annual statement has grown to impressive dimensions and at first sight may appear too formidable and complicated to repay the attention of the uninitiated. But this is not so. True, the *Blue Book* does not waste any space on general explanations, but it sets out the main aspects of the nation's housekeeping in a fairly simple and straightforward way: by how much the total income of the community changes from year to year; how it originates in the various branches of production; in what proportion it is made up of wages, salaries, profits, interest and rent; how it flows into different channels of private and public expenditure; how that part of it which goes to individuals is spent by them on consumption, paid in taxes or saved; how that part which goes to public authorities gets allocated among defence, education, the health service and other purposes; how investment is distributed over different industries and different types of capital good; and so on. In short, the *Blue Book* provides the background for most reviews of the economic situation in Britain, such as appear annually in the *Economic Reports* [40], and it is around it and its American counterpart, published by the U.S. Department of Commerce, that we shall work.

The plan of this book is as follows. Chapter I defines the national income and relates it to other totals of income and product. Chapter II introduces the basic concepts of production, consumption and accumulation and relates them to one another following the principles of an accounting system. Chapter III takes up the question of comparing totals of income and product over time. Chapter IV goes further still and discusses the problems of comparing income and product levels in different countries. Finally, Chapter V gives an outline of the more advanced forms of economic description which follow rather easily once the ideas of income, product and expenditure are understood. A list of works cited is given at the end of the book and the entries in it are referred to in the text by numbers enclosed in square brackets.

This short introduction to social accounting was written during 1960 in place of a fifth edition of Meade and Stone's *National Income and Expenditure* [20], which first appeared in 1944. Since social accounting hardly existed in 1944 and since the intervening years had also seen a great improvement in the statistics of national income and expenditure, we decided, in agreement with Professor Meade, that the time had come to give up revising the original version and to write a new one which would reflect these developments.

An eighth edition being now required, we have taken the opportunity to bring the figures as far as possible down to 1964. We have also added to Chapter III a section on quarterly statistics, which nowadays form an important part of national accounting both in Britain and in America, and on the problems of seasonal adjustment.

R. and G.S.

Cambridge
January 1966

CHAPTER I

WHAT IS THE NATIONAL INCOME?

1. *The National Income and Other Income Totals*

LET US begin by asking what the national income is. We all know, broadly, what we mean by an individual's income. He may receive it as a wage or a salary from his work, as a profit from his business, as rent from his property, as interest or dividends from his securities, as a pension or assistance grant from the state or from a public fund. Is the national income merely the sum of the incomes of all the individuals in the community?

The answer is no. The total of individual incomes, including the income of non-profit-making institutions, which are considered as aggregates of individuals, is usually called *personal income*. To this the qualification 'before tax' is sometimes added to indicate that taxes on income have not been deducted.

If we take the 1965 *Blue Book* [34] (to which we shall refer throughout) and look at table 2 we shall see that in 1964 total personal income amounted to £27,394 million. If we study the table we shall see that this figure relates to a concept of personal income which includes provisions for depreciation and stock appreciation. For the moment we shall not go into the meaning of these terms, but we shall see later that they are really out of place in a concept of income. At this stage we shall simply note that the figures for depreciation and for stock appreciation should be subtracted from personal income. They are not in table 2 of the *Blue Book* but can be obtained respectively from tables 58 and 66, and amounted in 1964 to £528 + 58 = 586 million. We shall also find it convenient to subtract the small amount of taxes paid abroad, £8 million. Personal income defined to exclude all these items is £27,394 − 586 − 8 =

[handwritten margin notes: aggregate, individual y's, given, personal income (before taxes)]

9

26,800 million. This is the figure for personal income which we shall adopt in this book.

Let us now return to our quest of the national income. Starting from the readily intelligible total of personal income we shall note, in the first place, that some elements of income never get distributed to individuals at all. The most important of these is the *undistributed income* of business corporations. These corporations make a profit and sometimes supplement it with income from other sources, but only a part of it all is distributed to the shareholders; the undistributed part is retained by the corporations and, after deduction of income and profits taxes, saved for the extension of their capital equipment or for building up their reserves of securities and cash.

If we begin by restricting corporations to *private* corporations (or companies, as they are called in the *Blue Book*), the sum of their undistributed income and of personal income gives a total of *private income*, again before tax. An estimate of this can be derived from table 3 of the *Blue Book*, which relates both to private companies and to public corporations. There it can be seen that the excess of the total income of companies (after remittances and taxes paid abroad) over total payments of dividends and interest (gross of British income tax) and transfers to charities amounted in 1964 to £3,939 million. As with personal income, this figure includes depreciation (except for companies operating abroad) and stock appreciation. Tables 58 and 66 show that the necessary deductions amount to £948 + 249 = 1,197 million. The undistributed income of companies in 1964 after these deductions was therefore £3,939 − 1,197 = 2,742 million, and so total private income was £26,800 + 2,742 = 29,542 million.

To this estimate of total private income we must now add the undistributed income of *public* corporations and any other income which accrues to the state from its productive activity and from the property it owns. Let us take these additional items one at a time. From tables 3, 58 and 66 of the *Blue Book* we can see that in 1964 the undistributed income of public corporations (before tax and including additions to interest

[margin notes: to P.I. add undistributed profits of private firms]

[margin notes: of public corporations (income to state from its property)]

reserves, but deducting depreciation and stock appreciation) amounted to £596 − 631 − 8 = − 43 million. From tables 43, 58 and 66 we can see that the trading and property income of the central government and local authorities amounted in the same year to £1,142 − 351 − 0 = 791 million. To this, in conformity with the *Blue Book*, we must add, from table 7, £20 million of British taxes paid by non-residents on portfolio income. Thus the income from productive activity accruing to public agencies of all kinds amounted in all to £ − 43 + 791 + 20 = 768 million. If we add this sum to the £29,542 million of private income, we reach yet another income total, £30,310 million.

Is this at last the national income? The answer is again no, because the national income is defined as the sum of all the incomes accruing to the inhabitants of a country, whether as wages, salaries, profits, interest or rent, from their contribution to production, and from this alone. So far we have not bothered to make a clear distinction between income derived from *productive activity* and income derived from *transfers* (or redistributions of income). But this distinction is fundamental because, as we shall see, the sum of all incomes earned in productive activity is precisely equal to the value of all products emerging from the productive system. One pound earned in wages by a man working in a motor-car factory or in dividends by a man who has contributed his capital to setting up the factory corresponds to a pound's worth of motor-car. If then the workman or the shareholder gives his pound to his godchild as a present, or to the state as a tax, and the state then perhaps passes it on to an old age pensioner, all that happens is that that bit of the country's total product is no longer enjoyed by the workman or the shareholder but by the child or the state or the old man. The value of the national product remains what it was before these transfers.

So the last step in reaching an estimate of the national income is to remove the transfer elements from the income totals derived so far. First, consider personal income. Gifts between persons, which are a form of transfer, are already cancelled out and do not appear in the *Blue Book*. Grants from public authorities, such as retirement pensions, sickness benefits, assistance grants and family allowances, must be deducted and these are shown in table 2 of the *Blue Book* to have amounted in 1964 to £2,362 million. This gives us a provisional total of £30,310 − 2,362 = 27,948 million.

Second, there is another form of transfer which at first sight does not look like one. This is *consumers' debt interest*, of which the classical example is the interest paid by the government on the national debt. Why, it may be asked, should this be excluded from the national income? Surely if interest received from businesses is included, should not interest received from consumers, whether these be private individuals or the government, be included too? The answer to this is no. If the proprietors of a business decide to borrow any additional money needed in their business instead of providing it from their own capital, then in future they will have to share the income yielded by their business with the people from whom they have borrowed, so that their profits will be diminished by the amount of interest they will have to pay; in other words, the income arising in the business in the form of interest and profits together is independent of the method of financing adopted. If we now apply these ideas to a consumer we see at once that, since consumption involves the using up and not the bringing forth of goods and services, no product and therefore no income from productive activity can arise in the course of consumption. Accordingly, consumers' debt interest must be treated as a transfer, or better still as positive income from productive activity to the lender which is matched by a corresponding reduction in the income from productive activity of the borrower, which is indeed how we shall treat it in section 8 of Chapter II. By either of these means the national income is made independent of past and present methods of financing consumers' expenditure in just the same way that it is automatically independent of methods of financing producers' expenditure.

In the *Blue Book* the estimates of income from rent, dividends and interest received by persons are given after deduction of certain interest payments made by persons, notably mortgage interest paid to building societies and interest on bank overdrafts. This treatment, which is the correct one, is not however uniform: interest on hire-purchase transactions, for instance, is not deducted, and as no figure is given for it in the *Blue Book* we must for the time being be content with an estimate of the national income slightly inflated by it. As to the debt interest paid by the central government and local authorities, this is shown separately in table 43 of the *Blue Book* and amounted in 1964 to £1,262 million. If this interest is subtracted from the provisional total given above there results £27,948 − 1,262 = 26,686 million.

This is in principle the *national income*. In practice, however, there is one small hurdle still to be surmounted. The estimates in the *Blue Book* are made from a large number of sources and some of the figures relate to incomes while others relate to expenditures. When they are finally brought together they do not exactly agree. As a consequence there is a small *residual error*, or statistical discrepancy, and by convention the compilers add this when positive to the sum of their direct estimates of total income and subtract it when negative. In 1964 this discrepancy was negative, − £234 million. The final figure for the national income in 1964 is therefore £26,686 − 234 = 26,452 million.

Summing up, the national income is the income which accrues to the inhabitants, or normal residents, of a country from their participation in world production. All such income is included, whether it is received by individuals in the form of wages, dividends, interest, etc., or is retained in private businesses, or accrues to government bodies as a consequence of their business activities. No other income is included; therefore gifts, grants and benefits, which are not received for participation in production, are excluded and so is consumers' debt interest. It does not matter where the income comes from: most of it will arise from production taking place within the country concerned, but some will arise abroad and will flow back to those who have provided the capital for undertakings abroad. In a corresponding way some of the income arising from production in the country will flow abroad to foreign shareholders, and so is excluded from the national income.

For many purposes, however, we need an income total which corresponds to the income arising from the productive activity that takes place within the territorial boundaries of a country, whether it accrues to the inhabitants of that country or not. Such a total is called *domestic income* and is obtained from the national income by subtracting *income from productive activity received from abroad* and adding *income from productive activity paid abroad*. According to table 7 of the *Blue Book*, in 1964, income (including taxes) received from abroad was £1,504 million, and income (including taxes) paid abroad was £1,099 million. Thus in 1964 the domestic income, as derived from the *Blue Book*, amounted to £26,452 − 1,504 + 1,099 = 26,047 million.

2. *The Net Domestic Product and Other Product Totals*

Domestic income is thus the sum of the incomes arising from the productive activity that takes place in a country, including the incomes distributed to foreigners in respect of their contribution to that activity. It provides a basis for valuing the production of a country and when considered from this point of view is called *domestic product* qualified as *net* and *at factor cost*. Let us see what these qualifications mean, and also what the reasons are for identifying income with product.

Goods and services have no abstract money value in themselves. We do not pay nature for accumulating large deposits of coal in the earth, or for stimulating the growth of pearls inside oysters, or for creating the human brain. When we speak therefore of the value of a good or of a service we mean the price we have to pay to induce human beings to bring forth these products for the enjoyment and enrichment of the community: the price we have to pay to induce, let us say, the miner to dig the coal out, the owner of capital to finance the necessary equipment, the owner of the land to allow his field to be dug up. Coal underground is worth nothing *per se*; nor for that matter is the pearl in the oyster or the latent ability of the poet or scientist. In order to bring into circulation these gifts of nature we need labour, capital and land. These are the three *factors of production*. Their contributions to production are called *primary inputs* and it is the rewards they receive for these inputs that constitute the first step in valuing what they produce. The sum of these rewards is the domestic income and it should now be clear why this is identical with the net domestic product at factor cost and why it is the fundamental valuation of what is produced in each country.

In producing goods and services, however, other expenses are incurred besides paying the factors of production. The *fixed assets*, such as buildings, ships and industrial equipment, needed for production are not everlasting and must be constantly renewed to keep production running steadily. The cost of these requirements is difficult to calculate exactly and the usual practice is to estimate it and set aside whatever sum seems likely to cover it. These provisions for the consumption of fixed assets are designed specifically to cover the wear and tear, in business language called depreciation, of capital equipment, its prospective obsolescence and any accidental damage to it. Commonly they go under the name of 'capital consumption' or of 'depreciation etc.', depreciation in the narrow sense of the word being by far their largest component, but in this book we shall refer to them simply as *depreciation*, dropping the 'etc.' and using the term in its general sense of loss of value. To get the full cost of products we must add depreciation to the incomes of the factors of production. We can see from table 1 of the *Blue Book* that depreciation in 1964 amounted to £2,458 million. If we add this to the net domestic product at factor cost we get £26,047 + 2,458 = 28,505 million, which is the *gross domestic product at factor cost*.

Are goods and services then sold at gross factor cost? The answer is no, because there are other elements that affect their value and consequently affect their *market price*; these are *indirect taxes* and *subsidies*. When we buy a packet of cigarettes for 4s. 6d., about 1s. 2d. of the price goes in factor costs and depreciation and 3s. 4d. goes to the government in indirect taxes. Conversely, when a miller buys a cwt. of wheat from a farmer at the market value of 20s., that wheat may well have cost the farmer 26s. to produce but he will not lose money by selling it below cost because the extra 6s. will have been provided by the government in the form of a subsidy. Thus if we add indirect taxes to a product total valued at factor cost and subtract subsidies from it we obtain the corresponding total valued at market prices. Again from table 1 of the *Blue Book* we see that indirect taxes or 'taxes on expenditure' amounted in 1964 to £4,457 million and subsidies to £520 million, which gives us a balance of £4,457 − 520 = 3,937 million, called *indirect taxes (net)*. If we add this to the gross domestic product at factor cost we get a total of £28,505 + 3,937 = 32,442 million which is the *gross domestic product at market prices*, or simply the *gross domestic product*.

Does this mean that in 1964 the British productive system turned out goods and services to the market value of £32,442 million? Superficially the answer is yes, but if we think over what we have said about depreciation we shall see that in fact it is no. The *final product* of a country falls into two main categories: those products which the community enjoys directly and uses up fairly quickly, namely consumption goods, and those more durable products which go to increase the capital wealth of the community, namely fixed assets, or investment goods. At first sight all new investment goods might appear to be an addition to the country's wealth, but we must not forget that in the course of producing both these and the consumption goods some of the existing capital equipment has worn out. Thus part of the fixed assets produced in a period should be considered as a replacement of those that have worn out during that same period; not a physical replacement, ship for ship, factory for factory, but a financial one, the value of the new assets making up for the deterioration of the old ones. Therefore to get a true, or net, measure of what a country has produced we must deduct depreciation from the gross domestic product. This will leave us with a total of final product, valued at market prices, composed only of consumption goods and of that part of investment goods which has actually increased the existing stock of assets, namely *net investment*, or 'additions to wealth'. The sum of consumption goods and net investment is the *net domestic product at market prices*. We have seen that in 1964 depreciation amounted to £2,458 million, and so the net domestic product at market prices for that year was £32,442 — 2,458 = 29,984 million.

The net domestic product at factor cost states the value of final product from the point of view of the producer. The net domestic product at market prices states it from the point of view of the buyer. The two gross product totals, at factor cost and at market prices, by including depreciation introduce among final product what is in fact a running expense and therefore an irrelevant element which belongs among the means of production, not among its ends. In principle, therefore, gross totals do not provide a true measure of product. In practice, however, they are more widely used than net ones because they are easier to calculate, as they avoid the tricky problem of measuring depreciation accurately. And since depreciation appears to be a fairly constant proportion of total product, gross totals are not too misleading for comparative purposes.

Having examined the meaning of these various product totals, let us now approach them by another route. If we think of the total production of a country, we think in the first place of all the products brought into being in that country over a certain interval of time, say a year. Some of these, such as raw materials, semi-finished products, fuels and business services, will be used in production. Others will be used by consumers, though they may be the same products, for instance coal, as are used by producers. Yet others, the fixed assets, will be accumulated and put to productive use in the future.

If we took every product produced in a year, valued it at its market price and added up the resulting sums of money we should obtain a total which might be regarded as a measure of the total value of production in the country. But this measure would be an unsatisfactory one because it would involve a large amount of duplication. For example, coal and iron are needed to make steel and therefore if we included in a country's total product both the value of the coal and iron used in the steel industry and the value of the steel produced, we should find that we had duplicated the value of that coal and iron, since their value is included in that of the steel they have contributed to produce. So to avoid duplication we must subtract the value of the *intermediate products* used in steel-making from the value of the steel produced. The difference between these two values is termed *value added* in steel-making, and the sum of the values added in each industry will give us a total of final product free of the duplication of intermediate product.

Let us now see what happens to value added. Most of it, in the form of wages, salaries, profits, interest and rent, goes to the factors of production as a reward for their primary inputs; a smaller part goes to the government in indirect taxes; and the remainder goes to provide for depreciation.

Thus we see that total value added is nothing but the gross domestic product. We know that it is a total free of duplication as far as intermediate products are concerned. But if we want a total free of all duplication, in the same way as we have subtracted the value of the current goods used up in production we should subtract the value of the capital goods used up for the same purpose; in other words, we should subtract depreciation. By subtracting depreciation from value added we get the net domestic product at market prices. Finally, if from this we subtract indirect taxes (net) we are left with that part of value added which is distributed among the factors of production. This is simply the net domestic product at factor cost.

So much for the domestic product. Many people prefer another definition of product, which excludes income paid abroad and includes income received from abroad. This is a national as opposed to a domestic concept and, as we have said, gives a measure of a country's productive activity irrespective of whether this activity takes place at home or abroad. When calculated to exclude depreciation and indirect taxes it is called the *net national product at factor cost* and is numerically identical with the national income; as in the case of domestic income and domestic product, it is simply a way of looking at the same total from a different point of view. If to this total we add depreciation we obtain the *gross national product at factor cost* (termed in the *Blue Book* 'gross national product' without other qualification). If to this we then add indirect taxes (net) we obtain the *gross national product at market prices* and this is the total which we, in accordance with the more widespread convention, shall call for short the *gross national product*. Calculated in this way, the gross national product in 1964 was £26,452 + 2,458 + 3,937 = 32,847 million. Alternatively, we can pass direct to it from the gross domestic product by adding to the latter income from productive activity received from abroad net of similar income paid abroad. This will give us a total of £32,442 + 405 = 32,847 million, as above.

Although the gross national product is the most widely used of product totals it should be approached with great circumspection. First, it has the defect of gross concepts, that it embodies under the form of depreciation a number of products which should be classed as running expenses. Second, it has the defect of national concepts when applied to product, that it cannot be identified with a collection of complete products: if a motor-car is produced in Britain by the co-operation of British labour and foreign capital, its value will be the sum of the incomes which the British landowner, the British workman and the foreign investor derive from its production, plus indirect taxes and depreciation, so that by excluding that part of income which goes to the foreign investor we are left with only part of the value of that motor-car; in the same way income from abroad will represent only a fraction of whatever product the British investor has contributed to produce abroad. Third, the gross national product only takes into account movements of income and does not make the corresponding adjustments for indirect taxes, subsidies and depreciation, and is therefore a hybrid total.

3. Taxes in the Valuation of Income and Product

It is now time we discussed the position of taxes in these concepts of income and product. Why, it may be asked, having defined domestic income as income from productive activity, did we exclude indirect taxes from it but did not exclude direct taxes? Before we answer this question let us name the more important taxes in each category. The principal indirect ones are: customs and excise duties on tobacco, drinks and petrol, protective import duties, purchase tax, motor licences, stamp duties and local rates. The principal direct ones levied on income are: income tax, surtax, profits tax and national insurance and health contributions.

As far as indirect taxes are concerned the list is self-explanatory: they must be excluded from domestic income because they represent a business cost which does not remunerate any input into the productive system. In order to make beer we need malt, hops, sugar, yeast and other intermediate products, we need the use of vats and other durable equipment the cost of which is measured by depreciation, and we need labour, capital and land whose remuneration constitutes domestic income arising in brewing. But we do not need, except in a purely legal sense, excise receipts for beer duty. The domestic income is intended to measure the income of all who contribute to domestic production and therefore the cost, in terms of factor rewards, needed to make that production possible. Evidently indirect taxes have no place in such a concept, whose importance can be seen from the following numerical example.

In Britain in 1964 private consumers spent £1,919 million on clothing and £2,661 million on drinks and tobacco. Of these totals, £119 million and £1,467 million respectively represent indirect taxes. Thus the payments to the factors of production, plus the provisions for depreciation, plus the imports required to satisfy these two categories of consumers' demand were £1,800 million and £1,194 million respectively. In other words, the relative resources involved, namely domestic factors, use of existing equipment and imports, were about 3 to 2, not the 3 to 4 that market values might lead us to believe.

This is the normal case. The payment of indirect taxes buys nothing which the branch of production concerned wants and nothing that it needs except a receipt. When the taxes get into the hands of the government they will no doubt be wisely spent to the great advantage of the community; but this has little or nothing to do with production. There may be abnormal cases, though we are unable to give a specific example. Thus it might happen that the government owned all durable equipment and instead of charging interest and depreciation to the industries in which this equipment was employed simply levied sales taxes, which over industry as a whole met depreciation and interest charges and also provided some net revenue. If such an unbusinesslike arrangement does exist anywhere in the world then evidently it is desirable to reckon the interest and depreciation charges embodied in this levy, subtract them both from it and include interest in the domestic income. Only thus shall we know what the resources used up in production have been. In short, we must always try to go behind the words to the underlying economic realities.

We come now to the second question: why is domestic income defined before the deduction of direct taxes? The answer is that incomes before tax are the amounts which have to be paid to buy the services of the factors of production. It is to be expected that the relative use of these factors in any branch of industry will be decided with reference to their relative prices; it is irrelevant to the producer that the owners of the factors transfer to the tax collector part of the price he must pay for their services.

To sum up, it is useful to have a product concept which excludes indirect taxes because these in no way represent a service to the production into whose cost they enter. Equally it is useful to have an income concept which includes direct taxes because the inclusive concept reflects the actual costs of different factors of production. Domestic income meets exactly these requirements, and the national income is simply the participation of the inhabitants of a particular country in the domestic income of the whole world.

4. *Some Recent Statistics of Income and Product*

Let us now pause and consolidate the position we have reached by reviewing the course of the national income and of other totals of income and product over the last twenty-five years. This is done in table 1 below for this country and for the United States of America.

Some interesting information can be obtained from this table. For example: in Britain in 1964 the undistributed income of companies before tax was nearly $9\frac{1}{2}$ per cent of private income, whereas in America it was about $8\frac{1}{2}$ per cent; in both countries government income from property was small throughout the period; in Britain, with its well developed social services and comparatively large national debt, transfers were nearly $12\frac{1}{2}$ per cent of private income as against less than 8 per cent in America; in Britain depreciation was nearly $9\frac{1}{2}$ per cent of domestic income as against nearly 11 per cent in America; in Britain indirect taxes (net) were a little over 12 per cent of gross domestic product as against $8\frac{1}{2}$ per cent in America.

If we look at the trends of the series in the two countries, the impression is that all the main totals have risen through time, the rise between 1938 and 1948 being particularly striking in America. But in making these comparisons we must remember that the estimates for different years are expressed in terms of the prices ruling at the time and not in terms of a fixed set of prices. In other words, while these money totals have been rising the value of money has been falling, and it is only if a money total has risen faster than the value of money has fallen that the corresponding total has risen in *real terms*. We shall come back to this problem in Chapter III.

If we try to compare the figures for the two countries, we run into a similar problem: the British estimates are expressed in pounds, the American in dollars. To make a comparison we

TABLE 1

The National Income and Other Totals of Income and Product

	United Kingdom £ million					United States* $ milliard (billion)				
	1938	1948	1954	1958	1964	1938	1948	1954	1958	1964
1. Personal income	4,996	9,718	14,023	18,241	26,800	69·6	213·9	295·9	370·1	512·8
plus Undistributed income of companies before tax	278	1,216	2,027	2,288	2,742	1·8	26·0	28·7	29·6	47·3
2. Private income	5,274	10,934	16,050	20,529	29,542	71·4	239·9	324·6	399·6	560·1
plus Government income from property†	78	-59	131	151	768	0·4	0·8	1·4	1·8	3·1
less Transfers	-536	-1,258	-1,712	-2,383	-3,624	-3·6	-15·1	-20·4	-30·3	-43·4
plus Residual error	0	61	128	287	-234	—	—	—	—	—
3. National income	4,816	9,678	14,597	18,584	26,452	68·2	225·7	305·6	371·1	519·8
plus Statistical discrepancy						0·6	-1·0	2·9	1·6	-0·5
less Income from abroad (net)	-192	-235	-249	-290	-405	-0·4	-1·0	-1·6	-2·0	-4·1
4. Domestic income (net domestic product at factor cost)	4,624	9,443	14,348	18,294	26,047	68·4	222·6	306·8	370·6	515·2
plus Depreciation	359	848	1,340	1,791	2,458	7·3	14·5	28·1	38·9	55·7
5. Gross domestic product at factor cost	4,983	10,291	15,688	20,085	28,505	75·7	237·2	334·9	409·5	570·9
plus Indirect taxes (net)	585	1,439	2,079	2,649	3,937	8·6	19·4	28·3	35·8	53·7
6. Gross domestic product	5,568	11,730	17,767	22,734	32,442	84·3	256·6	363·2	445·3	624·6
plus Income from abroad (net)	192	235	249	290	405	0·4	1·0	1·6	2·0	4·1
7. Gross national product	5,760	11,965	18,016	23,024	32,847	84·7	257·6	364·8	447·3	628·7

Components do not always add up to totals because of rounding-off errors.

* In conformity with the *Blue Book* (tables 1 and 7), includes British taxes paid by non-residents on portfolio income.

† In conformity with the *Blue Book* (tables 1 and 7), includes British taxes paid by non-residents on portfolio income.

need to know the relative purchasing power of the dollar and the pound. We also need to know the relative populations, since the comparison is most interesting when expressed as so much per head. At this stage we are not really in a position to make these calculations, but even so it is hard to resist doing sums on the back of an envelope. The population of America is three and a half times as large as the population of Britain. In terms of purchasing power, the exchange rate of £1 = $2·8 is usually believed to undervalue the pound: let us accept the common belief that £1 = $3·5 is nearer the mark. If we take the population factor and the purchasing power factor each as $3\frac{1}{2}:1$, we get a factor of 12·25 with which to multiply the British national income in order to compare it with the American. If we take 1964, we see that 519·8/(12·25 × 26·452) = 1·6 approximately. This means that if national income per head at equivalent purchasing power is taken as a measure of the relative standard of living, then in 1964 the Americans were about 60 per cent better off than the British. This is a crude comparison but we shall see in Chapter IV that it is not very wide of the mark.

5. *The Sources of the Statistics*

In concluding this chapter a word is needed about the sources of the figures. In the case of Britain, their derivation from the 1965 *Blue Book* has been given step by step for 1964. Most of the figures for the other years can be derived in the same way from the same issue of the *Blue Book*. Some of the earlier figures, however, can only be derived from earlier issues, and therefore do not reflect certain minor changes in coverage and definition introduced in later issues. For 1938 some of the bits are missing even from the earlier *Blue Books* and had to be obtained from unofficial sources.

In the case of America, at the time of preparing this edition the American estimates were undergoing one of their periodic major revisions. In describing the sources of the figures, therefore, we can no longer, as we did in former editions, refer to

U.S. Income and Output [51], issued in 1959 by the U.S. Department of Commerce as a supplement to the monthly *Survey of Current Business* [49]. Fortunately, however, almost all the figures we need can be derived from the national income and product tables published in the August 1965 issue of the *Survey* itself, and the few that are missing have kindly been supplied to us in anticipation of the new supplement, due to come out very shortly.

Returning to table 1, the derivation of the American figures is as follows. To obtain item 1 in our table, personal income, we must take line 16 of table 4, or more simply 4.16, in the *Survey*, add to it 4.10 and 4.11 and subtract 5.25. To obtain item 2 we must add 4.9 and subtract 4.14. To obtain item 3 we must add 9.32 (which unlike 7.30 we treat as a profit and not as an indirect tax) and subtract 4.12 and 4.13. To obtain item 4 we must add 4.6 and subtract 12.80. To obtain item 5 we must add 4.2. To obtain item 6 we must add 4.4 and subtract 7.30. Finally, if to this total we add back 12.80 we obtain item 7, the gross national product, which is identical with 1.1 in the *Survey*.

As to the principles on which these official publications are compiled, the conceptual framework of the British national income statistics and an account of the sources and methods used in estimating them are set out in *National Income Statistics: Sources and Methods* [35]. For America details of this kind are given in [51] and in the August 1965 issue of [49]. Both countries produce a large number of quarterly statistics which enable the national income picture to be kept up to date: the British estimates appear in *Economic Trends* [33], the American ones in [49]. The British government also issues each year at the time of the Budget a White Paper entitled *Preliminary Estimates of National Income and Balance of Payments* [36].

CHAPTER II

FROM NATIONAL INCOME TO NATIONAL ACCOUNTS

1. *Forms of Economic Activity*

IN THE preceding chapter we have distinguished between a number of totals of income and product and shown how to pass from one to the other. The time has now come to define the constituents of these totals and show how they are related to each other to form a closed network of flows. In doing this we shall gain some insight into the basic structure of an economic system.

An economic system is one in which goods and services are produced with the ultimate object of satisfying human wants. *Production* takes place in mines, farms, factories, shops, offices and other workplaces and, as we have seen, the total product of any period can be divided into two parts, intermediate product and final product.

Final product in its turn is divided into two parts: the first and largest flows into *consumption*, the second goes to maintain and increase the fixed assets needed by the productive system. It may happen that some of the products intended for inter- mediate or final consumption are not in fact consumed in the period in which they are produced and so form an *increase in stocks* which will be available at the end of that period for use in the future. This addition to wealth, whether in the shape of fixed assets or of an increase in stocks, is called *accumulation*. Since the whole of final product is either consumed imme- diately or is accumulated for the future, it follows that *final product equals consumption plus accumulation*.

Production, consumption and accumulation are the three basic forms of economic activity. Its ultimate aim is consump- tion, but since production requires the services of durable equipment it is necessary that this equipment should be maintained and increased if consumption is to be maintained and increased. If a large part of production is accumulated it is to be expected that the capacity to produce will rise so that in the future more products will be available for consumption. On the other hand if no part of production is accumulated it is to be expected that the capacity to produce will remain constant, and if the stock of durable equipment is not even maintained the capacity to produce will fall. In practice, of course, other forces, social, political, scientific or natural, may affect productive capacity, but, other things being equal, the larger the part of final product devoted to accumulation the larger will be future consumption as compared with present consumption.

All that has just been said relates to a *closed economy*, that is to say an economic system which is entirely isolated from other such systems. The economies of actual countries are never isolated in this way and transactions with other economies have to be considered. Thus the production of a given country is supplemented by imported products, and all the final product of a country is not exhausted by domestic consumption and accumulation but in part flows abroad in the form of exports. To trace such flows we must record not only all transactions connecting production, consumption and accumulation but also all transactions which the *rest of the world* has with the country we are considering.

If we record in four statements, or accounts, the *incomings* and *outgoings* relating to a country's production, consumption, accumulation and foreign transactions, we shall find that we have drawn up a closed network of flows which show the basic structure of an economic system and explain how most of the income and product totals of Chapter I fit into it. Only personal and private income will not emerge at once and the reason is that these two totals relate not to the economy as a whole but to institutional subdivisions, or *sectors*, of it. Once we have got the main structure clear we shall go into the question of sectors.

2. *Regions and Boundaries*

Since we are dealing with the structure of a system, some readers may find a simple geometrical analogy illuminating. We shall see in the next section that the idea of the *production boundary* is important and also that, just as we may think of production as a region cut off from the other forms of activity and from the rest of the world by a boundary, so we can apply the same idea to consumption, accumulation and the rest of the world.

We can represent the economy of the world by a closed region, say the interior of a circle. If we now draw a circle inside this region, the original circle will be divided into two parts, an outer ring and the interior of the inner circle. Let the outer ring represent the rest of the world and the interior of the inner circle represent the domestic economy. If we draw a second boundary which divides the interior of the inner circle into two parts we may identify production with one of these parts. If we draw yet another boundary which connects the inner circle with the second boundary and divides the second of the two parts in two, we may identify one of the new regions with consumption and the other with accumulation. Thus we can construct diagram 1 below.

In the following four sections we shall be concerned with the flows over the boundaries in the interior of this closed region. These flows will be expressed in terms of money due to be paid or received and not in terms of the goods, securities, tax demands etc., which flow the other way. Thus, for instance, the sale of goods from production to consumption will be represented by a flow of money from consumption to production, although the goods themselves flow in the opposite direction.

3. *Production: Domestic Product Account*

What flows over the production boundary are the incomings and outgoings associated with bringing goods and services into

DIAGRAM 1

Regions and Boundaries

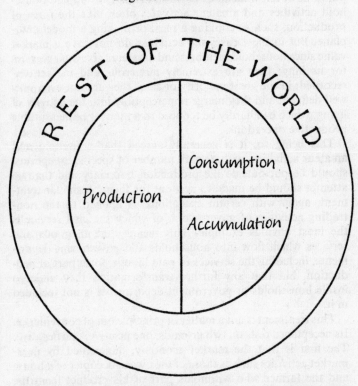

being. Before we try to classify these flows let us consider what we include in production.

If we consider a business which makes cars or clothes or bread, or renders services such as transport or dry-cleaning or running football pools, we shall not only want to include its output in production but we shall also find it easy to do so, since the products are well defined and sell at definite prices. The same may be said of all goods and services *produced for the market,* including that part which is not in fact sold but retained by the producer for his own consumption. Beyond this point, however, difficulties begin to arise. Thus unpaid household activities and amateur activities often take the form of production, such as cooking a meal or making a model aeroplane. But in these cases the activities do not have a market value since household members and amateurs give their services for nothing; they are extremely numerous and in fact unrecorded; in the great majority of cases they are not even very well defined; and they merge imperceptibly into the activity of living, which can hardly be reduced to a number of measurable productive operations.

This being so, it is generally agreed that household and amateur activities, with a small number of specific exceptions, should be put outside the production boundary and that no attempt should be made to account for them. A similar treatment, again with certain exceptions, is applied to the non-trading activities of government, of which the civil service is the most obvious example. This means that all goods and services which flow into households and government departments, including the services of paid labour, form part of production, but that any further transformation they undergo inside households or government departments is not included in it.

This treatment is not a matter of principle but of convenience. Its acceptance rests on two grounds, one positive, one negative. The first is that the market economy, augmented by near-market activities such as those of the owner-occupier of a house and the farmer who withholds part of his product from the market for consumption by his family, is an interesting and useful object of study in itself. The second is that attempts to extend the production boundary by valuing household and amateur activities come up against an almost complete lack of information, so that the estimates that could at present be made would neither be useful in a study of the market economy nor make any real contribution to the study of domestic and government activity.

In advanced economies, where the use of money and the division of labour are highly developed and where business units are in most cases clearly separated from households, the concept of production just outlined is comparatively easy to follow. This is not so in primitive economies, where these distinctions are blurred. Since this book draws its illustrations mainly from two of the most advanced economies in the world no more will be said here on this subject. The problem, however, is one which greatly concerns the organizations engaged in setting up international standards for defining and measuring national income and product. On this and other questions the O.E.E.C.'s *Standardised System of National Accounts* [23] and the U.N.'s *System of National Accounts and Supporting Tables* [44] and *Yearbook of National Accounts Statistics* [45] go far beyond this little introduction in matters of detail. In particular the U.N. publications, which try to standardize the national accounts of countries as diverse as the United States and Nigeria, have a good deal to say on a workable definition of the production boundary.

Let us now take a typical producer and enumerate the incomings and outgoings, or revenues and costs, connected with his production.

The main source of revenue is the sale of products. These sales may be made to: (i) other producers for purposes of current production; (ii) consumers, whether households, private non-profit institutions or departments of central and local government, for purposes of current use; (iii) other producers for purposes of maintaining or adding to their capital equipment; and (iv) the rest of the world. The first of these categories is intermediate product and the remaining three, identified respectively with consumption, accumulation and exports, are final product. Of course when the exports reach their destination they may be used in production abroad, but as far as the exporting country is concerned they leave its productive system and so are treated as final product.

A second source of revenue consists of the value of the increase in stocks: it may happen that more is produced in a period than is sold, in which case the stock of products in the hands of the producer, called *output stocks*, will be larger at the end of the period than it was at the beginning. And, since when we turn to the outgoing side of the account we shall find the costs incurred in production charged whether the output has been sold or not, there must be on the incoming side of the account an imputed source of revenue corresponding to the value of any increase in output stocks.

The last source of revenue is subsidies, which in Britain are particularly important in agriculture, certain food industries and housing.

On the cost side there is first the intermediate product bought either from other domestic producers or from abroad. If, however, during a period more intermediate product is bought than is used up in production, this excess will represent an increase in *input stocks* which must appear also on the incoming side of the account as an imputed source of revenue, just like the increase in output stocks.

A second item of cost is depreciation. This, as we have seen, represents the value of fixed assets deemed to be used up in current production and is therefore a proper charge against the value of that production before the gain derived from it can be determined.

A third item of cost is indirect taxes, or taxes on sales. From the producer's point of view this too is a cost and, like any other cost, must be set against his sales revenue before his gain from production can be determined.

If at this point we strike a balance we shall find an excess of revenue over costs. This excess represents the gain from productive activity which is available for distribution among the factors of production. From the point of view of the owners of the business, however, part of this distribution of gain will represent further costs, such as wages to be paid to employees and interest to be paid to bond-holders. Only when these costs have been met do the owners of the business get the profit which accrues to them from their productive activity.

If we draw up an account on the above lines for every producer in a country and add all these accounts together, the sales and purchases of intermediate product will be equal and so can be cancelled out. Subsidies, instead of being considered as an item of revenue, are simply treated as a reduction in costs and subtracted from indirect taxes. Conversely, imports, instead of being considered as a cost, are treated as a reduction in the revenue from exports. This leaves us with a total of revenue consisting of the proceeds of final sales to domestic buyers *plus* the value of the increase in stocks *plus* net exports, which is equal to the gross domestic product; if depreciation is subtracted from this, there results the net domestic product at market prices; if indirect taxes (net) are subtracted from this second total, there results the net domestic product at factor cost or domestic income, which is either retained in the country or paid abroad.

These transactions are set out for Britain and America in table 2.

We can see from this table that between 1938 and 1964 the value of the gross domestic product increased nearly six times in Britain and seven and a half times in America. These increases in value being largely due, as we have said, to higher price levels do not reflect proportionate increases in quantities. We shall see in the next chapter that, although the total product did increase in both countries, these increases were much smaller than the above figures suggest.

Therefore, what with the changes in the value of money over the last twenty-five years and the different currencies used in the two countries, table 2 and the three which follow it are not very useful for comparisons over time and space except where these comparisons take the form of ratios within countries. For example, we can see from table 2 that in 1938 gross domestic investment in fixed assets (item 1b) was 12 per cent of gross domestic product in Britain and 11$\frac{1}{2}$ per cent in America. In 1964 the corresponding percentages were 18 and 17$\frac{1}{2}$. Thus in both countries the percentage was higher in 1964 than in 1938, and at each date it was slightly higher in Britain than in America.

TABLE 2

Production

(Domestic Product Account)

	United Kingdom £ million					United States* $ milliard (billion)				
	1938	1948	1954	1958	1964	1938	1948	1954	1958	1964
1. Sales										
(a) Consumers (8) ..	5,166	10,371	15,283	19,048	26,745	74·6	200·7	299·8	368·5	507·3
(b) Capital purposes (13a) ..	656	1,422	2,552	3,478	5,802	9·7	45·7	64·8	78·1	108·0
(c) Abroad (net) (19) ..	-254	-238	-124	108	-631	0·9	5·4	0·2	0·2	4·5
2. Value of the increase in stocks (13b) ..	0	175	56	100	526	-0·9	4·7	-1·5	-1·5	4·8
Total incomings ..	5,568	11,730	17,767	22,734	32,442	84·3	256·6	363·2	445·3	624·6
3. Depreciation (11) ..	359	848	1,340	1,791	2,458	7·3	14·5	28·1	38·9	55·7
4. Indirect taxes (net) (7) ..	585	1,439	2,079	2,649	3,937	8·6	19·4	28·3	35·8	53·7
5. Domestic income to										
(a) Domestic sectors† (6a) ..	4,563	9,116	13,764	17,458	24,948	68·2	222·4	306·5	370·1	514·2
(b) Abroad (16) ..	61	327	584	836	1,099	0·2	0·3	0·4	0·5	1·0
Total outgoings ..	5,568	11,730	17,767	22,734	32,442	84·3	256·6	363·2	445·3	624·6

* Components do not always add up to totals because of rounding-off errors.
† Includes residual error (Britain), statistical discrepancy (America).

But even this kind of comparison needs to be handled with care. First, there is the question of classification. In each country this has remained unchanged throughout the twenty-five years under review and the figures in a series are in principle comparable, although it should be remembered that the earlier ones, because of the insufficiency of statistical data, are likely to be less accurate than the later ones. But between the two countries comparability is more difficult to ensure, as the headings do not always cover the same categories. To take again item 1*b* as an example, the American definition of investment in fixed assets is different from ours, as we include in it public as well as private investment whereas the Americans restrict it to the private sector, bracketing public investment with other government purchases of goods and services. Accordingly, to make the series more comparable between the two countries we have transferred the one item of government investment shown separately in the American accounts, namely new government construction activity, from government purchases to investment.

Second, there is the question of what basis of valuation is used. All the totals in table 2, on which the above percentages are based, are expressed at market prices, which means that indirect taxes are included. For our present comparative purpose it is impossible to express them otherwise since the Americans only give market price values, but if these same totals were expressed at factor cost the relative position of consumption and investment as percentages of domestic product would be slightly different: indirect taxes fall more heavily on consumption goods than on investment goods, so that valued at market prices consumption appears relatively larger and investment relatively smaller than they are when valued at factor cost; also, as indirect taxes are lighter in America than in Britain, any excess of the British over the American percentage for investment appears smaller at market prices than it would at factor cost.

Third, there is the question of the changes over time in the relative prices of goods. While almost all prices have risen in the last twenty-five years, those of investment goods have on the whole risen rather more than those of consumption goods. Thus some part of the increase in the percentages between 1938 and 1964 is due to the fact that investment goods were relatively more expensive at the second date and not to the fact that relatively more of them were being bought.

Finally, the structure of values is different in the two countries. In America, for instance, investment goods are relatively cheaper than in Britain, so that if we priced the components of the British domestic product at American values we should find the percentage for investment slightly lower than it is at British values.

These comments are only intended here as a warning. In Chapters III and IV we shall see how actually to make these calculations over time and space at constant values.

Before concluding this section a word is needed about the sources of the figures. Those for Britain all come from tables 1 and 7 of the *Blue Book* and their derivation is simple. Item 1*a* is equal to consumers' expenditure *plus* public authorities' current expenditure on goods and services; item 1*b* corresponds to gross fixed capital formation at home; item 1*c* is equal to exports and re-exports of goods *plus* exports of services *less* imports of goods and *less* imports of services. Item 2 corresponds to the value of the physical increase in stocks and work in progress. Item 3 corresponds to capital consumption. Item 4 is equal to taxes on expenditure *less* subsidies. Item 5*a* can best be obtained by subtracting capital consumption and property income (and taxes) paid abroad from the gross domestic product at factor cost; and item 5*b* corresponds to property income (and taxes) paid abroad.

The figures for America are derived as follows. Item 1*a* is the sum of 1.2 and 1.20 in the *Survey*, *less* the sum of 7.22 and 9.27, government expenditures on structures, which the *Survey* includes among government purchases of goods and services but which we treat as part of capital expenditure; item 1*b* is equal to 1.7 *plus* the sum of 7.22 and 9.27; and item 1*c* is equal to 1.17 *less* 12.80, net receipts of factor income from abroad, which the *Survey* includes with net exports. Item 2 is the same as 1.14. Item 3 is the same as 4.2. Item 4 is equal to 4.4 *less* 7.30. Item 5 is equal in total to item 4 of table 1 above and is divided between income paid to domestic sectors, *5a*, and income paid abroad, *5b*, with the help of information not provided in the *Survey*.

4. *Consumption: Income and Outlay Account*

Let us now turn to the flows over the consumption boundary. In the last section we have considered a country as a producer, setting out its accounts as a businessman would, with revenues and costs connected with production alone. In this section we shall consider it as a consumer, setting out its accounts as an individual would, that is showing where it gets its income from and how it disposes of it. In this form of account all the items which we have met in table 2 as costs for the producer are, with one single exception, sources of income for the consumer, in other words flow from production into consumption. The exception is the provisions for depreciation; these, being as we have seen a sum which the producer must set aside as a future source of finance for the replacement of his fixed assets, cannot be distributed as income to anybody but must flow from production directly into accumulation.

The main constituent of consumers' income is the income which accrues to a country from its productive activity at home and abroad, in other words the national income. In addition to this there is some income from indirect taxes, which is reckoned as usual net of subsidies.

And how does a country dispose of its income? Most of it is spent on buying goods and services. This is *consumers' expenditure*, an outgoing which flows directly into production; indeed we have met it in table 2 as the producer's biggest source of revenue.

A second and much smaller outgoing flows out to the rest of the world in the form of private remittances and government grants abroad, or *current transfers abroad*; these are shown net, that is after deduction of all similar remittances and grants received from abroad. Transfers, which are gifts, must not be confused with expenditure abroad, which consists of purchases of goods and services in foreign countries; these purchases abroad are treated for reasons of convenience as imports and are included, together with most other imports, in consumers' expenditure at home and thus find their way to the rest of the world through the production account.

The third and last item of consumers' outlay is *saving*, which is the excess of consumers' income over their expenditure and their transfers abroad. Saving flows from consumption into accumulation where it becomes, like provisions for depreciation, a source of finance for capital expenditure; it is important however to keep a clear distinction between provisions for depreciation, whose function is simply to maintain the country's wealth of fixed assets, and saving, whose function is to increase it.

In this way we obtain table 3, which relates to the income and outlay of Britain and America.

The most striking feature in this table is the course of saving. In 1964 nearly 11½ per cent of income was saved in both countries; in 1938 the corresponding percentages were 4 in Britain and 3½ in America. In considering the pre-war figures it should be remembered that, while by 1938 both countries had recovered from the depths of the great depression, there was still a considerable amount of unemployment, particularly in America. In considering the early post-war figures it should be remembered that the impossibility of buying many consumers' goods in wartime, coupled with the high rate of private saving during the war, produced a situation which was conducive to spending, particularly in Britain.

The sources of items 6a, 7 and 8 have already been given. For Britain, items 6b and 9 come from table 7 of the *Blue Book*; and item 10 can most easily be obtained by taking the figure for total saving before providing for depreciation and stock appreciation in table 6, subtracting from it stock appreciation and adding the residual error, which are given lower down in

TABLE 3

Consumption

(Income and Outlay Account)

	United Kingdom £ million					United States* $ milliard (billion)				
	1938	1948	1954	1958	1964	1938	1948	1954	1958	1964
6. National income from										
(a) Domestic production† (5a)	4,563	9,116	13,764	17,458	24,948	68·2	222·4	306·5	370·1	514·2
(b) Abroad (20)	253	562	833	1,126	1,504	0·6	1·3	2·0	2·6	5·0
7. Indirect taxes (net) (4)	585	1,439	2,079	2,649	3,937	8·6	19·4	28·3	35·8	53·7
Total incomings	5,401	11,117	16,676	21,233	30,389	77·4	243·0	336·8	408·4	573·0
8. Consumers' expenditure (1a)	5,166	10,371	15,283	19,048	26,745	74·6	200·7	299·8	368·5	507·3
9. Current transfers abroad (net) (17a)	8	67	5	68	186	0·2	0·7	0·5	0·5	0·6
10. Saving† (12)	227	679	1,388	2,117	3,458	2·6	41·6	36·5	39·4	65·1
Total outgoings	5,401	11,117	16,676	21,233	30,389	77·4	243·0	336·8	408·4	573·0

* Components do not always add up to totals because of rounding-off errors.
† Includes residual error (Britain), statistical discrepancy (America).

the same table, and finally subtracting depreciation, which is given in table 58.

For America, item 6b was filled in with the help of information not provided in the *Survey*. It should be noted that although items 5b, factor incomes paid abroad, and 6b, factor incomes received from abroad, are not shown separately in the *Survey*, their difference is given in 12.80, as we saw in the preceding section; it is this net figure which enabled us to pass from national to domestic concepts in table 1. Returning to the sources of table 3, item 9 is the same as 5.26 in the *Survey*; and item 10 can most easily be obtained as 11.11 *less* 4.2 *plus* the sum of 7.22 and 9.27 and *plus* 7.27, which we treat as a capital, not as a current, transfer.

5. *Accumulation: Capital Transactions Account*

We come now to the flows over the accumulation boundary. These are all flows of capital. The incomings are two: depreciation, flowing in from production, and saving, flowing in from consumption.

The outgoings are three. First comes *domestic investment*, which is divided between expenditure on fixed assets (*less* sales of existing assets) and investment in stocks. Next comes *foreign investment*, or the net increase in claims against other countries. If we subtract depreciation from domestic investment we obtain net domestic investment, or the net addition to the country's tangible wealth at home; and if to this net total we add foreign investment we obtain the increase in the country's wealth at home and abroad. The third outgoing is *capital transfers abroad*, which are shown after subtraction of similar transfers received from abroad.

These flows are set out for Britain and America in table 4.

In a general way these concepts seem straightforward enough, but when we come to examining the estimates available we shall find that they present peculiar difficulties and are only now emerging from a distinctly unsatisfactory state. We shall illustrate this by discussing: (i) the definition of fixed assets;

TABLE 4

Accumulation

(Capital Transactions Account)

	United Kingdom £ million					United States* $ milliard (billion)				
	1938	1948	1954	1958	1964	1938	1948	1954	1958	1964
11. Depreciation (3)	359	848	1,340	1,791	2,458	7·3	14·5	28·1	38·9	55·7
12. Saving† (10) ..	227	679	1,388	2,117	3,458	2·6	41·6	36·5	39·4	65·1
Total incomings	586	1,527	2,728	3,908	5,916	9·9	56·2	64·6	78·3	120·8
13. Domestic investment in										
(a) Fixed assets (1b) .. :	656	1,422	2,552	3,478	5,802	9·7	45·7	64·8	78·1	108·0
(b) Stocks (2)	0	175	56	100	526	-0·9	4·7	-1·5	-1·5	4·8
14. Investment abroad (18) ..	-70	164	121	330	-412	1·1	1·9	-0·4	-0·1	5·8
15. Capital transfers abroad (net) (17b)	0	-234	-1	0	0	0·0	3·8	1·8	1·8	2·2
Total outgoings	586	1,527	2,728	3,908	5,916	9·9	56·2	64·6	78·3	120·8

* Components do not always add up to totals because of rounding-off errors.
† Includes residual error (Britain), statistical discrepancy (America).

(ii) the treatment of durable goods not classified as fixed assets; (iii) the measurement of depreciation; and (iv) the distinction between investment in stocks and stock appreciation.

Fixed assets, as we have seen, are the durable goods used for the purposes of production. A factory and its machinery, a ship, a railway track, an office complete with furniture and typewriters, a fleet of taxis are all fixed assets. Natural resources become fixed assets from the moment they are put to productive use; thus a seam of coal or a piece of waste land are not fixed assets, but mines and cultivated fields are. Housing being defined as a productive activity, houses are fixed assets whether they are owned by a property company, a public authority, a private landlord or an owner-occupier. The purchase of fixed assets is charged against capital and is by far the biggest outgoing in a capital account; indeed it is the main object of accumulation.

But just as it is convenient to draw the production boundary to exclude certain productive activities, so has it been found convenient to draw the boundary round accumulation to exclude a certain number of durable goods: those bought for purposes which lie outside the production boundary, whose cost is included in consumers' expenditure, and those classified as replacement parts, which are treated as intermediate product.

Let us take the first category first. If we look at households and government departments we see that they own and use a large amount of durable equipment which does not contribute a revenue to production. Obvious examples of this are private cars and washing machines, which are consequently regarded as consumption goods. This is not a very satisfactory solution. And the problem becomes more difficult still in the case of public buildings, schools, roads, drainage systems and the like. Should we treat the purchase of such goods as current or capital expenditure, and if we are to draw the line somewhere, where should we draw it?

These questions are at the moment unsettled, but the tendency is, rightly, towards admitting more and more durable goods into the category of fixed assets. In Britain for instance, as we have seen, all capital goods acquired by public authorities, whether for productive purposes or not, are included in domestic investment, with estimates given for their depreciation. In America, on the other hand, they are treated as current expenditure together with all other government purchases, but a concession to their importance is made in so far as public works and buildings are concerned by giving a table which shows the composition of new public construction activity. In both countries, however, household durables, while kept distinct from non-durables, are included among consumption goods.

It would be much better to treat as fixed assets at least the major pieces of durable equipment bought by government and private consumers. The decision to do so, however, would involve more than just a revision of the boundary between consumption and accumulation. In terms of tables 3 and 4, having subtracted total expenditure on durable goods from consumers' expenditure (item 8) and added it to domestic investment in fixed assets (item 13a), it would then be necessary to divide it into two parts, one equivalent to the depreciation of existing durables, the other equivalent to consumers' net investment. The first could appear as a separate item of consumers' outlay, called perhaps 'consumers' depreciation', the second would be added to saving (item 10); and both would go to increase the incomings of the capital account (items 11 and 12) and thus balance the increase in domestic investment.

But this would be an extremely untidy and awkward solution because it would introduce some depreciation, whose place is among the costs of production, into the consumption account. To avoid this anomaly the boundary between consumption and production would have to be moved too, so as to recognize certain household and government activities as productive. This would admit all owners of durable goods into the production account, and the changes in tables 2, 3 and 4 would then be as follows. Total expenditure on consumers' durables would be switched in tables 3 and 4 from item 8 to item 13a, as above, and in table 2 from item 1a to item 1b. What we have called 'consumers' depreciation' would take its proper place in table 2 as an increase in item 3; at the same time, since it does represent that proportion of durable goods which has been consumed during the period, it would also be left as part of item 8 and would consequently be included in item 1a, thus balancing the increase in item 3. The value of consumers' net investment would be transferred to item 10, and so in table 4 items 11 and 12 would find themselves increased to match the increase in item 13a, as happened above.

Having recognized the owners of durable goods as producers and re-allocated accordingly the money they spend on the purchase and depreciation of these goods, we now ask ourselves whether we have in fact accounted for all the costs incurred and the gains realized in using them. The answer is that we have where actual flows of money are concerned, but not where invisible costs and gains are concerned. When a man buys a car he thereby foregoes the income he would get if he invested that part of his capital in bonds or shares or other interest-bearing property. This means that running his own car costs him in current expenditure not only the price of petrol and repairs but also the equivalent of the income he foregoes. It also means that the enjoyment or the practical advantage he gets from his car must represent to him a gain equivalent at least to that income. So to get a complete picture of the function of durable goods in the economy we should not only bring out their capital value in the national accounts but also try to calculate the hidden costs and gains which derive from owning them, since these costs and gains obviously affect other branches of the economy, especially the service trades. The simplest way to do this would be to impute to the owners of durable goods, as is done for owner-occupiers of houses, an expenditure and an income equal to the interest on the capital value of those goods, reckoning this interest at the current rate. If this were done, items 1a and 5a of table 2 and items 6a and 8 of table 3 would be increased by the amount of the imputation.

Let us now turn to the second category of durable goods excluded from accumulation, namely replacement parts.

Replacement parts may be individually extremely durable; nevertheless their cost, together with that of the labour needed to install them, is treated as a current expense and appears as an outgoing in the production account for the year in which they are bought, like intermediate product. This treatment is often extended to whole pieces of equipment such as typewriters, which in a large concern will be bought on a regular annual basis. Its justification is that the separate items of expense are small, numerous and not readily postponable, so that with minor variations in composition they tend to recur year by year.

In accounting terminology this is the renewals method of treating the maintenance of assets as opposed to the depreciation method. When it is employed, as it sometimes is, to the exclusion of depreciation it works well in normal circumstances but not in abnormal ones. A good example of this is the maintenance of the permanent way of railways. These works can be regarded as virtually everlasting provided they are regularly attended to. This maintenance expenditure is treated as a current cost of operating the railway and the problem of depreciating the permanent way does not arise. It may happen, however, that under the pressure of financial losses, say, or of a war the railway company is forced to put its maintenance service on an emergency basis and carry out only the repairs which are essential for immediate needs. If this is done without introducing into the production account some provision for the abnormal deterioration which will inevitably ensue, then the true cost of operating the railway during the emergency period is underestimated and its profit is correspondingly over-estimated; also, the company's assets are represented in a misleading way since the track is in an abnormal state of disrepair and to put it right some extra expenditure of capital will be necessary in the future. Whereas if provisions for depreciation are introduced at the outset of the emergency, the true balance of costs and profits through time will be respected and the company will not find its capital resources strained when normal activity is resumed.

This brings us to the third question we undertook to examine, namely the measurement of depreciation. Three elements are necessary to calculate the depreciation of an asset: an estimate of its useful life, an estimate of the rate at which it will wear out and the price at which to value each successive stage of this wearing out.

Estimates of life can never be certain, if only because technical change may force replacement earlier than expected. However, a great deal of information is available about the life-span of different types of asset, so that in estimating the useful life of well-established types, past experience is quite a good guide. But with new types, where either the design or the materials or both have not been tested by use, the estimates can be little more than a guess.

Estimates of the rate at which assets wear out can be made in many different ways. The two methods most commonly followed are the straight-line method and the reducing-balance method. With the straight-line method, use is assumed to take place uniformly throughout the life of the asset, so that an asset whose life has been estimated at, say, ten years loses each year one-tenth of its full value. With the reducing-balance method a fixed proportion of the depreciated value of an asset is assumed to be used up in each period; thus if the proportion has been fixed at 20 per cent a year, then the asset loses 20 per cent of its value in the first year, 16 per cent (which is 20 per cent of its depreciated value) in the second year, 12·8 per cent in the third, and so on.

As to the price at which to value each successive stage in the depreciation of an asset, it is usual in private accounting to value it in terms of the original cost of the asset. This practice has the drawback that the prices of capital good, as of everything else, are subject to change and in the last generation have tended fairly steadily upwards. Accordingly, a better estimate of the current cost of using an asset is reached if the depreciation of the year is valued not at original cost but at current, or replacement, cost. Thus if in a particular year the price of an asset whose life-span is estimated at ten years has risen by 50 per cent then, supposing the straight-line method to be applied, the depreciation charge for that year should be not 10 per cent but 15 per cent of the original cost, which is equal to 10 per cent of the replacement cost.

The important point to keep in mind about depreciation is that however it is calculated it can at best express no more than a reasonable expectation of the cost of using durable equipment. Events may turn out differently from what had been expected and in this case a capital gain or loss will be made. Often when a piece of equipment becomes obsolete before the end of its estimated life, the whole of the outstanding depreciation is charged in one lump against revenue in the production account for the year in which the asset was scrapped, so that it appears as a reduction in profits, whereas it is a capital loss and should be treated as such. Conversely, if a fully depreciated asset is still in use beyond the estimated time, it represents a capital gain and should not be treated, as it often is, as an increase in profits. These and all similar unpredictable gains and losses of capital should appear in the capital account. Unfortunately, with the data we have at present any record we could give of these fluctuations of value would be too incomplete to be significant, and so for the time being it seems wiser to leave them all out.

We come now to the fourth question on our list: the difference between investment in stocks and stock appreciation. Investment in stocks represents the increase that has taken place during the period in the quantity of stocks held by the productive system. In section 3 of this chapter we have seen that if production is greater than sales there will be an accumulation of output stocks, and if more materials are bought than are used in the period there will be an accumulation of input stocks. Also there will always be at the end of a period a certain amount of work in progress, which can be thought of as stocks of un-finished product. All these accumulated stocks will eventually become a source of revenue to production: the output stocks will be sold as they are, the input stocks will be transformed into finished product, the work in progress will be completed.

Until they have actually been sold, however, this revenue can only be a notional one; what in fact happens is that some capital, instead of being invested in fixed assets, is tied up in holding these stocks of finished and unfinished product. This is why the value of the physical increase in stocks is also called investment in stocks and is represented as an outgoing in the capital account (table 4, item 13*b*) and an incoming in the production account (table 2, item 2).

But how is this physical increase to be estimated? If the opening value of stocks is subtracted from the closing value the difference will show the total increase that has taken place in the value of stocks during the period. This increase, however, may be due quite as much to an increase in the prices of the goods stocked as to an increase in their quantity, and is not therefore the figure we want. To get the required estimate we must take the increase in the quantity of each type of stock and multiply separately each increase by the average price fetched over the period by that particular kind of good. The sum of these products will give us the value of the increase in stocks. It may happen that in a period the quantity of stocks has fallen instead of rising, in which case investment in stocks will appear as a negative figure.

Stock appreciation, on the other hand, reflects the increase, also either positive or negative, that has taken place during the period in the prices of the goods held in stock. The simplest way of calculating it is to subtract investment in stocks from the total increase in the value of stocks. This will give us a figure for stock appreciation reckoned at the average prices of the period.

If positive, stock appreciation is a capital gain, if negative, a capital loss; in either case its place is among capital transactions and not among sources of income. We have excluded it altogether because, as we said above, it seems pointless to introduce in our accounts one comparatively unimportant item of capital appreciation when we cannot introduce any of the others. In the *Blue Book* stock appreciation is included in income from property, but it can easily be removed as a separate figure is given for it immediately below that for domestic income in table 1. In the *Supplement* this subtraction is performed by the compilers by means of the 'inventory valuation adjustment'.

The sources for items 11, 12 and 13 have already been given. For Britain, item 14 corresponds to net investment abroad in table 7 of the *Blue Book*, and item 15 is obtained from the same table by adding together capital grants from overseas governments (net) and other capital transfers from abroad. For America, item 14 is the same as 11.13 in the *Survey*, and item 15 is the same as 7.27.

6. *The Rest of the World: Balance of Payments Account*

Table 5 below brings together the transactions which Britain and America have with the rest of the world. In other words it is a condensed statement of the balances of payments of the two countries. Of course where Britain is concerned America is part of the rest of the world, and *vice versa.*

The entries in this table have all appeared in one or other of the three preceding ones, where they were presented from the point of view of the two countries concerned. Here they are seen from the point of view of the rest of the world, so that incomings and outgoings have their position reversed. The purpose of the table is not to set up a system of international accounts but merely to tie up the loose ends of tables 2, 3 and 4, hence the mixture of income flows and transfer flows and of current and capital transactions. The arrangement of the entries has been chosen for convenience in consolidating this table with the others, as we shall see in the next section.

7. *The National Accounts*

Tables 2, 3, 4 and 5 constitute a complete set of national accounts for Britain and America. Their essential unity is seen more easily if the figures for one country in one year are brought

4

TABLE 5

The Rest of the World

(Balance of Payments Account)

	United Kingdom £ million					United States* $ milliard (billion)				
	1938	1948	1954	1958	1964	1938	1948	1954	1958	1964
16. Income from British (American) production (5b)	61	327	584	836	1,099	0·2	0·3	0·4	0·5	1·0
17. Transfers from Britain (America)										
(a) Current (net) (9)	8	67	5	68	186	0·2	0·7	0·5	0·5	0·6
(b) Capital (net) (15)	0	−234	−1	0	0	0·0	3·8	1·8	1·8	2·2
18. Borrowing from Britain (America) (14)	−70	164	121	330	−412	1·1	1·9	−0·4	−0·1	5·8
Total incomings	−1	324	709	1,234	873	1·5	6·7	2·2	2·7	9·5
19. Imports from Britain (America) (net) (1c)	−254	−238	−124	108	−631	0·9	5·4	0·2	0·2	4·5
20. Income from productive activity to Britain (America) (6b)	253	562	833	1,126	1,504	0·6	1·3	2·0	2·6	5·0
Total outgoings	−1	324	709	1,234	873	1·5	6·7	2·2	2·7	9·5

* Components do not always add up to totals because of rounding-off errors.

together on one page. This is done for Britain in 1964 in table 6 below.

This table shows the structure of an economic system reduced to its simplest terms. The only distinctions made are between production, consumption and accumulation and, in the treatment of income, between income from productive activity and income from transfers. Into this framework all transactions in the system can be fitted by further subdivisions of accounts and entries. The statement is incomplete in only one respect: it relates only to flows and therefore, while it shows the additions to the country's wealth which have taken place during the period, it ignores the accumulated wealth which already existed at the opening of the period. In other words it does not contain a balance sheet. In Chapter V we shall see what the functions of a balance sheet are and why it is not possible at present to include one in the national accounts.

The headings and the numbering of the entries in table 6 follow exactly those in the preceding four tables. Each item appears twice, with the number of the corresponding entry shown in brackets after the heading. Thus item 1a corresponds to item 8, item 1b corresponds to item 13a, and so on.

The accounts in a closed system like that presented in this table can be combined in many different ways, with interesting results. For instance, if we consolidate the accounts for consumption, accumulation and the rest of the world, that is to say if we turn them into one and strike out the common entries, namely income from productive activity abroad (items 6b and 20), current and capital transfers abroad (items 9 and 17a, and 15 and 17b), investment abroad (items 14 and 18) and saving (items 10 and 12), we obtain an account for the gross domestic product which is identical with the production account except that incomings and outgoings are reversed: what is a source of revenue inside the production boundary becomes an item of expenditure outside it, and what is a cost to production becomes a source of revenue either to consumption or to accumulation or to the rest of the world.

Similarly, if we consolidate the accounts for production and

TABLE 6

National Accounts of the United Kingdom in 1964
(£ *million*)

Production
(Domestic Product Account)

1. Sales			3. Depreciation (11)	2,458
(*a*) Consumers (8)	26,745		4. Indirect taxes (net) (7) ...	3,937
(*b*) Capital purposes (13a)	5,802		5. Domestic income to	
(*c*) Abroad (net) (19) ...	—631		(*a*) Domestic sectors* (6a)	24,948
2. Value of the increase in			(*b*) Abroad (16)	1,099
stocks (13b)	526			
Total incomings	32,442		Total outgoings	32,442

Consumption
(Income and Outlay Account)

6. National income from			8. Consumers' expenditure (1a)	26,745
(*a*) Domestic production*			9. Current transfers abroad	
(5a)	24,948		(net) (17a)	186
(*b*) Abroad (20)	1,504		10. Saving* (12)	3,458
7. Indirect taxes (net) (4) ...	3,937			
Total incomings	30,389		Total outgoings	30,389

Accumulation
(Capital Transactions Account)

11. Depreciation (3)	2,458		13. Domestic investment in	
12. Saving* (10)	3,458		(*a*) Fixed assets (1b) ...	5,802
			(*b*) Stocks (2)	526
			14. Investment abroad (18) ...	—412
			15. Capital transfers abroad	
			(net) (17b)	0
Total incomings	5,916		Total outgoings	5,916

The Rest of the World
(Balance of Payments Account)

16. Income from British pro-			19. Imports from Britain (net)	—631
duction (5b)	1,099		(1c)	
17. Transfers from Britain			20. Income to Britain from	
(*a*) Current (net) (9) ...	186		British productive activity	
(*b*) Capital (net) (15) ...	0		abroad (6b)	1,504
18. Borrowing from Britain (14)	—412			
Total incomings	873		Total outgoings	873

* Includes residual error.

the rest of the world, items 1c and 19 will cancel out and so will items 5b and 16; and if we then consolidate the accounts for consumption and accumulation, item 12 will cancel item 10, and we shall have another pair of identical accounts with incomings and outgoings reversed. This pair will show the composition of the gross national product, consisting on one side of the national income *plus* indirect taxes (net) *plus* depreciation, and on the other side of consumers' expenditure *plus* investment at home and abroad *plus* current and capital transfers abroad.

These two examples illustrate the rule that if the accounts in a closed system are consolidated into two groups the two resulting accounts will be mirror images of each other.

The totals thus obtained, however, may not always be so significant as the two we have reached in our examples. To get a worthwhile total it may sometimes be necessary to adopt a process slightly more complicated than simple consolidation. Let us suppose, for instance, that we want to find out how much the inhabitants of a country have consumed and how much they have added to their wealth. To this end, having chosen the accounts which look most appropriate, namely consumption and accumulation, we must first consolidate them; this will give us, as we have seen, the gross national product, composed on the outgoing side of consumers' expenditure (item 8) *plus* investment at home and abroad (items 13a, 13b and 14) *plus* transfers abroad (items 9 and 15). The next step is to get rid of these transfers, which is done by moving items 9 and 15 to the other side of the account, changing their signs. This will leave us with a total composed of consumers' expenditure and gross investment, so that the final step is to subtract depreciation from it; this is done by moving item 11 to the other side of the account, of course changing its sign. Thus we shall reach on the outgoing side a total composed of expenditure on consumption goods (item 8) and net investment (items 13a, 13b and 14 *less* item 11), and on the incoming side we shall have the flows of income which finance this consumption and this investment, namely the national income and indirect taxes, net of our gifts to foreigners (items 6*a*, 6*b* and 7 *less* items 9 and 15). The same result in reverse will be obtained by performing the corresponding operations on the accounts for production and the rest of the world.

By such means we can readily discover the identities between sets of transactions which follow from the system of definitions we have proposed.

8. *Sectors*

The *Blue Book* and the *Supplement* contain a large number of detailed tables on which we have not touched and shall not touch in this little book. They all fit, however, into the framework we have developed and are obtained by taking the national accounts to pieces in different ways. Thus the domestic product account can be subdivided by industries, or by regions, or by legal forms of organization such as companies, unincorporated businesses, public corporations, and so on.

These subdivisions are the *sectors* of the economy. An important distinction is that between the private and the public sector, that is between individuals, non-profit-making institutions and private companies on the one hand and public corporations and the departments of central and local government on the other. As an example of how one of our tables can be expanded we shall now set out a consumption account for each of these two sectors.

Table 7 below gives the income and outlay of the private sector for Britain and America.

In this table we have taken the opportunity of including some additional details not shown in table 3. Thus that part of income from productive activity which represents the private sector's share of the national income is subdivided into three types of income, the last of which is in its turn divided between the amount received by persons (individuals and non-profit-making institutions) and the amount retained by companies. One item, however, income from productive activity abroad, no longer appears as a separate entry: it is included in items 1*c* (i) and (ii), following the *Blue Book*, which does not specify how it is distributed among the various domestic sectors but only gives the total figure for it. On the other hand, as a result of separating the private from the public sector a new item, benefits and grants received from public authorities, makes its appearance under the heading of *income from transfers*.

The outgoings of the account, with the exception of current transfers abroad, are also subdivided and expanded. Private consumers' expenditure is broken up into a number of commodity groups and saving is divided between persons and companies. Here too a new item appears, *taxes on income*, again as a consequence of separating the sectors.

As to the sources of the figures, for Britain they are to be found as follows. Item 1*a* corresponds to total income from employment in table 2 of the *Blue Book*; item 1*b* is equal to total income from self-employment in table 2 *less* the personal sector's depreciation on assets other than dwellings in table 58 and *less* the personal sector's stock appreciation in table 66; item 1*c* (i) is equal to rent, dividends and interest in table 2 *less* the sector's depreciation on dwellings in table 58; and item 1*c* (ii) is simply the undistributed income of companies as we have defined it in Chapter I. Items 2*a* and 2*b* correspond to total grants to persons in tables 36 and 40 respectively. The subdivisions of consumers' expenditure in items 3*a* to *h* all come from table 18 and can easily be traced there. Item 4 corresponds to transfers abroad (net) in table 2. Item 5*a* corresponds to national insurance and health contributions in table 2; items 5*b* and 5*c* correspond to payments of taxes on income in tables 2 and 3 respectively. Item 6*a* is equal to saving *plus* additions to tax reserves, both in table 2, *less* the personal sector's total depreciation and stock appreciation in tables 58 and 66; and item 6*b* is equal to undistributed income plus additions to dividend reserves *plus* additions to tax reserves, all in table 3, *less* the depreciation and stock appreciation of companies in tables 58 and 66.

For America, item 1*a* is the same as 3.2 in the *Survey*; item 1*b* is the same as 5.9; item 1*c*(i) is equal to the sum of 5.12, 5.13

TABL

Income and Outl

	United Kingd £ million		
	1938	1948	19
1. Income from productive activity†	4,999	10,229	15,0
(a) Wages etc.	3,022	6,785	10,2
(b) Earnings of the self-employed	613	1,154	1,4
(c) Interest (net), profits and rent			
(i) received by persons	1,086	1,074	1,3
(ii) retained by companies	278	1,216	2,0
2. Income from transfers	275	705	1,0
(a) Benefits and grants from central government‡	250	667	9
(b) Benefits and grants from local government‡	25	38	
Total incomings	5,274	10,934	16,0
3. Consumers' expenditure	4,394	8,615	12,1
(a) Food	1,285	2,210	3,7
(b) Drink	285	802	7
(c) Tobacco	177	764	8
(d) Clothing	446	902	1,2
(e) Housing	518	787	1,0
(f) Major durable goods			
(i) household	..	310	6
(ii) vehicles	..	48	2
(g) Public transport	167	357	4
(h) All other	..	2,435	3,2
4. Current transfers abroad (net)	0	26	–
5. Taxes on income	493	1,932	2,6
(a) Social security contributions	109	335	5
(b) Income tax and surtax paid by persons	292	971	1,2
(c) Income tax and profit taxes paid by companies	92	626	8
6. Saving†	387	361	1,2
(a) Persons	201	−229	
(b) Companies	186	590	1,1
Total outgoings	5,274	10,934	16,0

* Components do not always add up to totals because of rounding-off error
† Does not include residual error or statistical discrepancy.

the Private Sector

58	1964	United States* $ milliard (billion)				
		1938	1948	1954	1958	1964
45	27,180	69·0	229·4	309·6	375·5	525·9
58	19,577	45·0	141·1	208·0	257·8	365·3
80	1,980	11·3	40·2	40·0	46·6	51·1
19	2,881	10·9	22·1	33·0	41·6	62·1
88	2,742	1·8	26·0	28·7	29·6	47·3
84	2,362	2·4	10·5	14·9	24·1	34·2
98	2,215	1·2	7·6	11·5	19·5	27·8
86	147	1·2	2·9	3·4	4·6	6·5
29	29,542	71·4	239·9	324·6	399·6	560·1
73	21,334	63·9	173·6	236·5	290·1	398·9
47	5,557	15·6	46·3	56·5	66·6	79·9
11	1,317	3·3	7·9	8·9	9·8	12·4
31	1,344	1·7	4·0	4·9	6·0	7·8
54	1,919	8·0	24·2	26·8	29·9	40·0
47	2,246	8·9	17·5	31·7	41·1	59·5
50	1,001	1·9	7·7	10·5	11·7	16·6
25	854	1·4	7·1	13·5	15·1	25·5
22	691	1·2	3·0	3·0	3·1	3·6
86	6,405	21·9	55·9	80·8	106·8	153·5
-4	23	0·2	0·7	0·5	0·5	0·6
44	4,945	5·3	37·7	59·0	74·5	111·4
59	1,444	2·0	5·2	9·8	14·8	27·8
96	2,709	2·3	20·0	31·5	40·6	56·0
89	792	1·0	12·5	17·7	19·0	27·6
16	3,240	2·0	28·0	28·5	34·5	49·2
17	1,290	1·2	14·5	17·6	24·0	29·6
99	1,950	0·7	13·5	11·0	10·5	19·7
29	29,542	71·4	239·9	324·6	399·6	560·1

Here and in the following tables central government = federal government in e U.S., and local government = state and local government in the U.S.

and 5.14 *less* 5.25 and *plus* 4.15; and item $1c$(ii) is equal to 3.18 *less* 3.22. Item $2a$ is the same as 7.26 and item $2b$ is the same as 9.30. Item 3 is the same as 1.2, but the details are based on information not given in the *Survey*. Here we should say that our categories do not always follow the American classification of private consumers' expenditures but are roughly matched, in the interests of comparability, with those of the *Blue Book*; hence, for instance, the considerable difference between our figures for major durables and the American ones for all durables, which in 1964 amounted to $58·7 milliard as opposed to the $42·1 milliard given by us.

To return to our list of sources, item 4 is the same as 5.26 in the *Survey*. Item $5a$ is the same as 4.10; item $5b$ is equal to 5.21 *less* the sum of 7.5 and 9.4, which are treated by us as paid out of capital rather than income account; and item $5c$ is the same as 3.20. Item $6a$ is equal to the sum of 4.11, 5.27, 7.5 and 9.4; and finally item $6b$ is equal to the sum of 3.23 and 3.24.

Let us now pass on to the public sector. The income and outlay of this sector are set out in table 8 below.

The arrangement of this table is similar to that of table 7. In setting out income from productive activity, interest paid is deducted from interest received, that is the interest on government debt is treated as negative income to the government. It appears, of course, as positive income to the recipients, whether public or private, and so cancels out in the national income except for that part of it which goes abroad, whose positive counterpart is in the rest of the world.

Income from transfers consists of indirect taxes (net) and taxes on income. The former are exactly as in table 3. The latter are subdivided to show the net receipts of the three sub-sectors of the public sector. Public corporations have negative receipts since they pay but do not receive taxes on income; thus the totals in row $2(b)$ represent the taxes on income paid by the private sector.

These two categories of taxes are by far the most important but they do not make up quite the whole of the government's revenue from taxation. The missing element is *taxes on capital*, mainly death duties, which together with taxes on income make up *direct taxes*. These capital taxes are treated by us as capital transfers and so disappear in the consolidated account for capital transactions (table 4). The consequence of this treatment is that private saving is reckoned before paying these taxes and public saving is reckoned before receiving them.

The outlay side of table 8 shows public expenditure and public saving each suitably subdivided. It also contains the benefits and grants made to persons. Like taxes on income, these benefits and grants cancel out when tables 7 and 8 are consolidated.

If now the remaining subtotals in the two tables are added up and the statistical discrepancy added to income on one side and to saving on the other, the resulting items will correspond exactly to those in table 3.

For Britain the sources of the figures in table 8 are as follows. Item 1a is equal to total allocation of income in table 3 of the *Blue Book* *less* interest payments in the same table and *less* the depreciation and stock appreciation of public corporations in tables 58 and 66; item 1b is equal to gross trading income *plus* rent, dividends and interest *less* debt interest, all in table 4, *less* the relevant depreciation and stock appreciation in tables 58 and 66 and *plus* taxes paid by non-residents on portfolio income in table 7; item 1c is equal to gross trading income *plus* rent, dividends and interest *less* debt interest, all in table 5, *less* the relevant depreciation in table 58. Item 2a (i) is the excess of taxes on expenditure over subsidies, both in table 4, and item 2a (ii) is the excess of rates over housing subsidies in table 5; item 2b (i) is the negative of payments of taxes on income in table 3, and item 2b (ii) is the sum of taxes on income and national insurance and health contributions in table 4 *less* taxes paid by non-residents on portfolio income in table 7; item 2b (iii) is blank because in Britain local authorities do not levy taxes on income. Items 3a (i) and (ii) correspond respectively to military defence and to health services in table 36, and item 3a (iii) is obtained from the same table by subtracting these two items from total expenditure

TABl

Income and Outl

	United Kingdom £ million			
	1938	1948	1954	1!
1. Income from productive activity†	−183	−612	−560	−
(a) Public corporations..	−4	−118	−57	−.
(b) Central government‡	−194	−437	−435	−
(c) Local government ..	15	−57	−68	
2. Income from transfers				
(a) Indirect taxes (net) ..	585	1,439	2,079	2,0
(i) Central government	378	1,136	1,639	2,0
(ii) Local government	207	303	440	6
(b) Taxes on income ..	493	1,932	2,624	3,!
(i) Public corporations ..	0	−3	−37	−
(ii) Central government‡ ..	493	1,935	2,661	3,!
(iii) Local government	—	—	—	
Total incomings	895	2,759	4,143	5,4
3. Consumers' expenditure ..	772	1,756	3,113	3,6
(a) Central government ..	454			
(i) Military defence ..	..	740	1,520	1,4
(ii) Health service	..	185	470	6
(iii) Other	..	298	335	4
(b) Local government	318			
(i) Education	..	211	358	5
(ii) Other	..	322	430	5
4. Benefits and grants to persons ..	275	705	1,021	1,4
(a) Central government ..	250	667	967	1,3
(b) Local government ..	25	38	54	
5. Current transfers abroad (net) ..	8	41	15	
6. Saving†	−160	257	−6	2
(a) Public corporations..	−4	−121	−94	−2
(b) Central government ..	−177	409	117	4
(c) Local government	21	−31	−29	−
Total outgoings	895	2,759	4,143	5,4

* Components do not always add up to totals because of rounding-errors.

† Does not include residual error or statistical discrepancy.

	United States* $ milliard (billion)				
964	1938	1948	1954	1958	1964
494	−0·8	−3·7	−4·0	−4·4	−6·1
−43	—	—	—	—	—
385	−0·6	−4·3	−5·0	−5·6	−8·4
−66	−0·2	0·5	1·0	1·2	2·3
937	8·6	19·4	28·3	35·7	53·7
879	1·6	7·3	8·6	8·8	11·8
058	6·9	12·1	19·7	27·0	41·9
945	5·3	37·7	59·0	74·5	111·4
−8	—	—	—	—	—
953	3·9	34·4	53·1	65·8	95·8
—	1·5	3·3	5·9	8·7	15·6
388	13·1	53·4	83·3	105·8	159·1
411	10·7	27·1	63·3	78·4	108·4
930	..	..	37·1	40·5	..
941	..	..	..	..	..
657	..	..	..	..	..
929	..	..	8·0	12·4	..
954	..	..	11·3	16·4	..
362	2·4	10·5	14·9	24·1	34·2
215	1·2	7·6	11·5	19·5	27·8
147	1·2	2·9	3·4	4·6	6·5
163	0·0	0·0	0·0	0·0	0·0
452	0·0	15·7	5·1	3·3	16·4
−51	—	—	—	—	—
382	−1·9	12·3	−1·8	−6·2	−0·7
121	1·9	3·5	6·9	9·5	17·1
388	13·1	53·4	83·3	105·8	159·1

In conformity with table 1 above, British taxes paid by non-residents ortfolio income are included in government income from property 1b) and therefore excluded from taxes on income (item 2b (ii)).

on goods and services; item 3*b* (i) corresponds to education in table 40, and item 3*b* (ii) is equal to all other expenditure on goods and services in the same table. Item 4*a* corresponds to national insurance benefits and other current grants to persons in table 4, and item 4*b* corresponds to current grants to persons in table 5. Item 5 is equal to current grants paid abroad *less* current grants from overseas governments in table 4. Item 6*a* is equal to total allocation of income in table 3 *less* payments of interest and U.K. taxes on income in the same table and *less* depreciation and stock appreciation in tables 58 and 66; item 6*b* is equal to the surplus in table 4 *less* depreciation and stock appreciation in tables 58 and 66; and item 6*c* is equal to the surplus in table 5 *less* depreciation in table 58.

As to the American sources, items 1*a*, 2*b* (i) and 6*a* are left blank because public corporations do not appear in the *Survey* as a separate category but are treated as part of central and local government. Item 1*b* is the negative of 7.29, and item 1*c* is equal to 9.32 *less* 9.31. Item 2*a* (i) is equal to 7.9 *less* 7.30; item 2*a* (ii) is the same as 9.10; item 2*b* (ii) is equal to the sum of 7.2, 7.8 and 7.18 *less* 7.5; and item 2*b* (iii) is equal to the sum of 9.2, 9.9 and 9.22 *less* 9.4. Item 3 is equal to 1.20 *less* the sum of 7.22 and 9.27, but the revised details are not available in the *Survey*. Item 4*a* is equal to 7.26 and item 4*b* is equal to 9.30. Item 5 is zero in every year because net government transfers to foreigners are treated by us as capital transfers. Item 6*b* is equal to the sum of 7.22, 7.27 and 7.31 *less* 7.5; and finally item 6*c* is equal to the sum of 9.27 and 9.33 *less* 9.4.

CHAPTER III

COMPARISONS OVER TIME

1. *Product Totals at Constant Prices*

IF WE look at item 6 of table 1 above we can see that between 1958 and 1964 the gross domestic product of the United Kingdom rose from £22,734 million to £32,442 million, that is to say it increased in value by 43 per cent. But without more information this comparison is not very enlightening, since we do not know how far the rise was due to more products and how far it was due to higher prices. Accordingly we must now try to find out by how much the gross domestic product changed in quantity over the period 1958 to 1964.

Let us suppose that we know the quantity of each of the products which constituted the gross domestic product in 1958 and in 1964 and, further, that each product produced in one year was also produced in the other. With these data we could compile a set of quantity ratios expressing the final output of each product in 1964 in terms of the corresponding final output in 1958. The problem then is: how are we to average these ratios? We could simply add them up and divide their sum by the number of final products, but this would not be very satisfactory since a big item like bread would contribute no more to the answer than a small item like birdseed. One way of getting over this difficulty would be to weight the ratio for each product by the relative importance of that product in the total output of 1958. If we added up the weighted ratios and divided by the value of total output in 1958 we should obtain what is called a weighted average of the ratios, to which each ratio would contribute in proportion to the value of the corresponding product in 1958.

Before we go any further let us be quite clear about the type of calculation that has just been described, since it forms the basis of almost all practical comparisons of product and price levels over space and time. Consider a community that lives on bread and cheese and keeps pet birds. The entire final product of this community consists of bread, cheese and birdseed. The prices, quantities and values of these three commodities are assumed to have been as follows in two periods which we wish to compare:

	Base period (period 0)			Current period (period 1)		
	Price (£ per ton)	Quantity (tons)	Value (price × quantity)	Price (£ per ton)	Quantity (tons)	Value (price × quantity)
Bread	20	100	2,000	30	90	2,700
Cheese	50	10	500	40	15	600
Birdseed	10	10	100	25	20	500
Total	...	...	2,600	...	...	3,800

The changes in the quantities of the three products relative to period 0 are respectively $90/100 = 0.9$, $15/10 = 1.5$ and $20/10 = 2.0$. If we multiply, or weight, each quantity ratio by the corresponding value in period 0 as shown in the table and add up the resulting numbers, we obtain $(2000 \times 0.9) + (500 \times 1.5) + (100 \times 2.0) = 2750$. If we now divide this sum by the total value in period 0, we obtain $2750/2600 = 1.058$ approximately. This is the weighted average of the ratios. We could obtain the numerator even more simply by multiplying the quantities in period 1 by their respective prices in period 0 and adding up the resulting numbers. Thus $(20 \times 90) + (50 \times 15) + (10 \times 20) = 2750$ as before.

Thus, according to this calculation, total product was higher in period 1 than it was in period 0 by 5.8 per cent in *real terms*. That the increase should work out to some such small figure is intuitively plausible since while the consumption of cheese and birdseed went up considerably, the consumption of bread, which is much the biggest constituent of total product, actually fell by 10 per cent. This shows the importance of weighting; if we had taken a simple average of the quantity ratios we should have obtained $(0.9 + 1.5 + 2.0)/3 = 1.467$ approximately, indicating a rise in quantity of 46·7 per cent. This result is absurd, being larger than the rise in the value of total product in spite of the substantial increases in the prices of bread and birdseed.

The obvious comment on the estimate of 5·8 per cent for the rise in total product is that there is no particular reason for using the values of period 0 as weights in preference to the values of period 1. If we did the calculation the other way round we should have to take the sum of the quantities of period 0 each multiplied by its respective price in period 1 and divide this total by the sum of the values in period 1. To compare period 1 with period 0 on this basis we should then have to take the reciprocal of this ratio. This alternative estimate is $3800/[(30 \times 100) + (40 \times 10) + (25 \times 10)] = 1·041$. So on this basis the total product of period 1 was only 4·1 per cent higher than the total product of period 0. Since we have no reason to prefer one estimate to the other we might say at this point that the true increase probably lies between 4·1 and 5·8 per cent; and since for practical purposes we shall often want a single figure, we can easily obtain one by averaging the two estimates.

So far we have concentrated on the average change in quantities. Suppose now that we turn our attention to the average change in prices. This can be determined by the same technique which we have applied to quantity changes. And, quite apart from the intrinsic interest of such calculations, we shall see that they also provide an alternative approach to the measurement of quantity changes, since if the average price change is divided into the change in the total value of product it will give precisely the quantity measure which we have derived above by a more direct route.

2. Index-numbers of Prices and Quantities

Let us now see why this is so by setting out the formulae we have just described for average changes in quantities and in prices. Estimates based on such formulae are called *index-*

5

numbers. They may take many mathematical forms; those described are called *aggregative index-numbers* and are the most commonly used because they are easy to understand, simple to calculate and possess a number of other convenient properties.

In the conventional symbolism of index-numbers, prices and quantities are denoted respectively by the symbols p and q, to which is added the suffix 0 or 1 according as they relate to the base or to the current period. The usual sign for summation, Σ, is used to denote the sum of the values which constitute a product total. Each of these values has the form of price multiplied by quantity. Thus $\Sigma\, p_0 q_0$ denotes the sum of base-period quantities each multiplied by its price in the base period, and $\Sigma\, p_1 q_0$ denotes the sum of base-period quantities each multiplied by its price in the current period. In terms of the numerical example given in the last section $\Sigma p_1 q_0 = (30 \times 100) + (40 \times 10) + (25 \times 10) = 3650$.

The typical quantity ratio relating the current period to the base period is q_1/q_0. If each such ratio is multiplied by the corresponding value in the base period and if the resulting numbers are added together and divided by the sum of the values in the base period, we obtain

$$\frac{\Sigma\left(p_0 q_0 \cdot \dfrac{q_1}{q_0}\right)}{\Sigma p_0 q_0} = \frac{\Sigma p_0 q_1}{\Sigma p_0 q_0} \qquad \ldots (1)$$

This is Laspeyres' formula for an index-number of quantities and may be denoted by Q_L. From the left-hand side of (1) this index-number can be regarded as a base-weighted arithmetic average of quantity ratios. From the right-hand side of (1) it can be regarded as the current product total revalued at base-period prices divided by the actual value of the base-period product total.

If in (1) we interchanged the 0's and 1's we should get similar expressions in which the role of base and current periods had been interchanged. If we then took the reciprocals of these expressions we should return to our original base and so should obtain another index-number comparable with (1). It would have the form

$$\frac{\Sigma p_1 q_1}{\Sigma \left(p_1 q_1 \cdot \dfrac{q_0}{q_1} \right)} = \frac{\Sigma p_1 q_1}{\Sigma p_1 q_0} \qquad \ldots \text{(2)}$$

This is Paasche's formula for an index-number of quantities and may be denoted by Q_P. From the left-hand side of (2) this index-number can be regarded as a current-weighted harmonic average of the quantity ratios q_1/q_0. From the right-hand side of (2) it can be regarded as the actual value of the current product total divided by the base product total revalued at current prices.

The formulae in (1) and (2) are measures of the average change in quantities. Corresponding measures of the average change in prices can be obtained by interchanging the p's and q's. Thus from (1) we obtain

$$\frac{\Sigma \left(p_0 q_0 \cdot \dfrac{p_1}{p_0} \right)}{\Sigma p_0 q_0} = \frac{\Sigma p_1 q_0}{\Sigma p_0 q_0} \qquad \ldots \text{(3)}$$

This is Laspeyres' formula for an index-number of prices and may be denoted by P_L. Similarly from (2) we obtain

$$\frac{\Sigma p_1 q_1}{\Sigma \left(p_1 q_1 \cdot \dfrac{p_0}{p_1} \right)} = \frac{\Sigma p_1 q_1}{\Sigma p_0 q_1} \qquad \ldots \text{(4)}$$

This is Paasche's formula for an index-number of prices and may be denoted by P_P. The alternative interpretations of P_L and P_P follow exactly those of Q_L and Q_P.

If we denote by V the ratio of the current to the base product total, that is $\Sigma p_1 q_1 / \Sigma p_0 q_0$, then it is easy to see that

$$P_L\, Q_P = P_P\, Q_L = V \qquad \ldots \text{(5)}$$

In other words, if properly combined these measures of average price-change and average quantity-change multiply out to the change in value, just as would happen with a single commodity. But to achieve this result the measures must be mixed, one being of type L and the other of type P. Single measures can be obtained on these lines by taking the geometric average of the two price index-numbers as a measure, P_F say, of the average price-change and by taking a similar average, Q_F say, of the two quantity index-numbers. Thus

$$P_F = \sqrt{P_L P_P} \qquad \ldots (6)$$

and

$$Q_F = \sqrt{Q_L Q_P} \qquad \ldots (7)$$

and so, as is easily verified,

$$P_F Q_F = V \qquad \ldots (8)$$

These index-numbers, P_F and Q_F, are Fisher's *ideal index-numbers* for prices and quantities.

If we return for a moment to the numerical example given in the preceding section, we can set out the change in value, V, the three index-numbers of prices, P_L, P_P and P_F, and the three index-numbers of quantities, Q_L, Q_P and Q_F, as follows:

$$
\begin{aligned}
V &= 1 \cdot 462 \\
P_L &= 1 \cdot 404 \\
P_P &= 1 \cdot 382 \\
P_F &= 1 \cdot 393 \\
Q_L &= 1 \cdot 058 \\
Q_P &= 1 \cdot 041 \\
Q_F &= 1 \cdot 049
\end{aligned}
$$

The reader should have no difficulty in checking these results and in verifying the relationships (5) and (8) above for this example.

Many other forms of index-number have been devised. A systematic account of most of them has been given by Fisher in [10] and new suggestions are constantly appearing. However, as we have already said, the above forms are simple and convenient and we shall not go beyond them.

3. *Measures of Individual Prices and Quantities*

We have seen that the comparisons we can make are affected numerically by the formula used, but so long as we rely on well-established types of index-number we can be confident that in practice we shall not obtain freakish and misleading results. We have also seen that our comparisons are affected by the choice of base year. In actual cases this choice will often be determined by practical considerations such as the availability of data or the desire for comparability with other series. But, in so far as we have a choice, we should remember that relative prices stand for relative valuations by consumers or producers and we should therefore try to choose a period when these are normal. This means that we should try to avoid a year which contains a general strike, a failure of the harvests or the onset of depression because we may expect that in such years many markets will be seriously out of equilibrium so that relative prices and relative quantities will be unrepresentative.

With a little care, therefore, these problems are not serious. The real difficulty in constructing index-numbers is to obtain enough accurate information on the movement of individual prices and quantities.

We have seen that the data needed to construct price index-numbers are the same as are needed to construct quantity index-numbers and so in the following brief account we shall concentrate on the latter. In order to compare total product in two years we must subdivide the total value according to products and measure the quantity change of each component. Most of the information readily available on quantities is expressed in simple units such as number, weight, volume or area. But these simple units often mask a considerable diversity in quality, model and other characteristics which affect prices and costs. They ought therefore to be scrutinized very carefully. In doing this the guiding principle to be followed is that similar articles which sell at different prices are *prima facie* different; if further scrutiny confirms this assumption, they should be either treated separately or measured in units such that the prices per unit of the different varieties are approximately equal to one another. Let us look at some typical problems in the light of this principle.

(1) *Quality differences.* Consider the case of eggs, by which we mean hens' eggs. These are usually graded by size and freshness, and different grades sell at different prices. Now, eggs are usually recorded by number. This is a satisfactory indicator of quantity only when there has been no change between the periods under comparison in the average size and freshness of the eggs sold, but when there has been a change we should like it to be reflected in the comparison. If from the available statistics we could distinguish between eggs of different grades, we could treat each grade as a separate commodity, weight it by its own price and everything would be straightforward. Unfortunately the basic data are most unlikely to be available in this detail, but sample information or even the impressions of poultry keepers and distributors may enable us to adjust the crude quantity comparison, provided we know the relationship between price and quality in the base period.

Another example is provided by beer. In this country the quantity of beer is measured in bulk barrels, which reflect the amount of liquid, and standard barrels, which reflect the amount of alcohol. If the beer becomes stronger the standard measure will rise more than the bulk measure. Typically the statistics give two totals for the whole output of beer, one in bulk and the other in standard barrels, without distinguishing among different qualities, so that we cannot treat beers of different strengths as separate commodities. But we can work out the relationship between price and strength in the base period and this will tell us how best to combine the two quantity indicators we have. Incidentally, if we have to choose one unit or the other there can be no doubt that we should choose standard barrels.

(2) *New Models.* In the case of many manufactured goods quality changes are introduced to the public by means of new models, with the consequence that similar products made in different years are different. A good example of this are motor-

cars. These are typically recorded by number. But their performance, economy, reliability and comfort change very much from period to period as new models are thought up. In principle we could find out how these characteristics were related to price in the base period and then adjust the crude measure in numbers according to the changes that have taken place in these characteristics. In practice, however, it is difficult to compare periods which are not close together: in order to price modern cars at 1910 values it would be necessary to extrapolate the price-quality relationship of 1910 beyond the ranges of quality that were then available. As a short cut we might note the fact that generally speaking the price of cars within each period is closely related to their weight. Thus even a rough estimate in tons would be superior to an accurate estimate in numbers, because most of the desirable features of a car are positively associated with weight. But new technical developments may change this and so weight may become a misleading substitute for the qualities that affect price.

(3) *Composite products and fixed charges.* This problem is well illustrated by the case of goods transport. The volume of traffic is usually recorded in ton-miles with some subdivision by commodity. Ton-miles are frequently taken as the quantity indicator for goods transport, but in fact charges are not as a rule proportional to ton-miles since the goods have to be loaded and unloaded, an expense which is independent of distance and in some cases quite considerable. The relationship between the total charge per ton and the distance makes it possible to disentangle the constant part of the charge from the part which varies with distance. The former should be associated with a quantity indicator expressed in tons and the latter with one expressed in ton-miles. If we assume that the total charge per ton is equal to a fixed charge independent of distance plus a constant rate per mile multiplied by distance, we can see that if the fixed charge is zero then we need only an indicator expressed in ton-miles; while if the rate per mile is zero, so that the total charge is independent of distance, then we need only an indicator expressed in tons.

The same idea can be applied to passenger travel, with the number of passengers taking the place of tons of merchandise. We may find that the charge per passenger is a fixed sum independent of distance and in this case the proper quantity indicator is the number of passengers. Or the charge per passenger may be proportional to distance and in this case the proper quantity indicator is the number of passenger-miles. From this we see that the proper indicator depends on the structure of the charges in operation. If this structure changes between the two periods, then the indicator to be used will be that proper to the base period.

The same situation arises when charges are made under a two-part tariff, as frequently happens, for instance, with electricity. In these cases the consumer pays a fixed charge plus a constant charge per unit of current. Electricity consumption is usually measured in units of current (kilowatt-hours), but it would be better if the total expenditure on fixed charges were associated with an indicator of the number of consumers and only the balance of the expenditure were associated with an indicator of the quantity of current consumed.

(4) *Trade and transport charges.* Some farm products, like fresh vegetables, may be consumed by the growers or they may be taken to city markets and sold at prices far exceeding those received by the growers, the difference being made up of trade and transport charges. Accordingly, farm consumption and city consumption should be kept separate because the price per ton is appreciably different in the two cases.

It is sometimes argued that this is all wrong because a cabbage is a cabbage whether it is consumed by a farmer or a townsman and that if anything it is rather more of a cabbage, and so should be weighted more heavily, if it is consumed by a farmer because in that case it is likely to be fresher. But this argument overlooks the fact that people choose to live in towns and that transport and distributive services are necessary to make this possible. If between two periods there has been a move from country to town, we must recognize the fact that in the later period the community has chosen to devote rather more resources to trade and transport and rather less to growing cabbages, and we should allow this fact to be reflected in our comparison of final product. Although we shall not go into such details here, it can be seen from [27] how it is possible to set out the calculations so as to show in what measure cabbages, trade and transport contribute respectively to the change in final product as a whole.

(5) *Seasonal variations.* Seasonal commodities provide another example of similar goods selling at widely different prices. During their season, strawberries are cheap and consumed in large quantities; out of season they are very expensive and very few are consumed, or they may be altogether unobtainable. The question now is: is a strawberry always a strawberry or are winter strawberries a different commodity from summer ones? According to the guiding principle of this section they are undoubtedly different commodities. This means that we should not treat the annual consumption of strawberries as a single component of final product with a single average price but we should try to treat strawberries consumed in different seasons as different commodities each with its own average price. The seasons can be grouped in any way provided that the price within a season is relatively constant. If a single annual indicator is required for the quantity of strawberries consumed, the appropriate one is the sum of the quantities in each season of the current year each multiplied by the normal seasonal level of strawberry prices in the base year divided by the corresponding quantities in the base year each multiplied by the same factor.

Of course if the seasonal pattern of consumption does not change between the two periods under comparison, these more refined calculations will give the same result as crude ones. But in fact the seasonal pattern does change, partly because with rising incomes people can afford more 'out of season' varieties and partly because technical developments such as refrigeration are constantly at work to reduce the price and so increase the consumption of 'out of season' varieties. The effect of such technical progress shows in the refined calculations but not in the crude ones: in all cases where seasonal luxuries have come down in price the consequent rise in consumption will appear higher when weighted by the prices of the earlier period than when weighted by those of the later period.

(6) *Bewildering variety.* In some cases individual articles are produced in a bewildering number of qualities and types and the materials and designs used are constantly changing. Clothing illustrates this problem well. Let us take two simple examples, men's shirts and women's stockings. We might be able to discover the number of shirts bought in each period to be compared, but this would be a crude indicator of quantity since there might have been important changes in quality. If we tried to divide shirts into different categories we should probably find that the information was not available, and even if it were we should have to face the difficulty that some of the categories did not exist in the base period.

The best thing to do in such cases is to approach the measurement of quantity change through the construction of price index-numbers. In doing this we should concentrate on pricing certain specific articles defined as narrowly as possible in terms of quality, and rely on the fact that goods made of similar materials and by similar processes would probably move in price in approximately the same way as the articles we had chosen as samples. Then by measuring the change in expenditure and dividing it by the price index we might hope to get an improved measure for the change in quantity. For instance, if shirts are either relatively cheap cotton ones or relatively expensive silk ones, the price index might show no change, the total number of shirts bought might show no change either, but the expenditure on shirts might have increased: this would indicate that people were now buying relatively more silk shirts and relatively fewer cotton ones than in the base period, in other words that the average quality of shirts had risen, a fact which would be reflected in the ratio of the change in expenditure to the change in the price index-number.

It must be remembered that in practice difficulties are seldom encountered singly, and it may well happen that some of the difficulties discussed above will be superimposed on the problem of bewildering variety. Thus a change in raw materials may make it very hard to continue a price series of constant quality because the popular article selected for pricing in the base year has been largely replaced by a similar article with different characteristics. The substitution of nylon stockings for silk ones is a case in point: if a pair of nylon stockings lasts perceptibly longer than a pair of silk ones, then the pair ceases to be a satisfactory unit and we are back at the problem discussed at (2) above.

This summary of the difficulties of defining suitable units leaves many questions unanswered. A fuller treatment will be found in the O.E.E.C. report on index-numbers [27] which has already been referred to. The only thing to be added here is that it is from attention to basic details of the kind discussed in this section more than from debates on formulae or base periods that improvements are likely to come.

4. *Final Product and Value Added at Constant Prices*

So far, the product totals we have had in mind have been totals of final product, namely the gross domestic product and its components. Before we leave this field we should recall our earlier discussion of the production boundary in which we decided to put all activity in households and government outside that boundary, with a small number of specific exceptions. When we come to quantity comparisons this means that the quantities we are trying to measure for these sectors are the quantities of goods and services, including the direct services of labour, which households and government departments buy. This in turn means that the final product associated with, say, education is to be measured in real terms by reference to what goes into education and we do not have to consider what comes out of it any more than we have to consider what households do with food, string, paper hats and all the other things they buy.

At first sight this may seem unsatisfactory but reflection will

show that it is less unsatisfactory than the practicable alterna-
tives. For how should we construct a quantity indicator for
education? Should we take the number of students, or the total
number of marks gained in national examinations, or what?
Any such measure would be inferior to a measure based on
inputs since, despite Parkinson and his law, there can be no
doubt that more teachers, larger class rooms, more equipment
and greater facilities give us the best approximation we can get
to more education; it may not be a very good one but it is
better than the number of students or the number of marks.

We have already seen that, for the economy as a whole, total
final product is identically equal to total value added. This is
evident in table 2 above (p. 34), the upper half of which shows
the different categories of final product while the lower half
shows the components of total value added. These components
could be subdivided by industry and then added together
industry-wise to give total value added in each industry. These
industrial values added are composed of primary inputs,
depreciation and indirect taxes, or of primary inputs alone if
we value final products at factor cost and net.

Suppose now that we try to compare the value of primary
inputs in terms of constant prices. We might approach this
problem by trying to find quantity indicators for primary
inputs, but once we had done the calculation for labour we
should find the other factors of production, namely capital and
land, much more difficult to handle. In fact little has been
achieved in this field, but if the calculation could be done it
would provide a measure of the quantity of primary inputs
which when divided into the quantity of output would show the
change in productivity of all primary inputs taken together.

There is, however, an entirely different approach which
allows the whole calculation to be carried out by revaluing
products. Value added is the excess of the value of an industry's
output over the value of the intermediate products, which we
shall here call intermediate inputs, consumed by that industry.
If the quantities in the current period are all revalued at the
prices of the base period and if, for each industry, the revalued

intermediate inputs are subtracted from the revalued output, there results a set of measures of value added at base-period prices which can be compared with the actual values added in the base period.

This measure of value added at constant prices corresponds to value added as net output rather than as primary input. The interesting thing is that if values added at base-period prices are summed over all industries the same figure is reached as when final products at base-period prices are summed over all industries. The reason for this is not difficult to see: starting with the total value of output in each industry, to get final product we subtract that part of the industry's output which goes to other industries (its output of intermediate product), and to get value added we subtract in each case the product of other industries which goes to the industry in question (its input of intermediate product). When we sum these calculations over all industries we have in each case the value of all goods and services produced less the value of all intermediate product. This identity is true whatever prices are used and so the domestic product account balances at constant as well as at current prices. We may therefore show the gross domestic product at constant prices either as the sum of all final products emerging from the productive system or as the sum of all values added in different branches of production.

In principle, the value added calculation as we have described it is that used for index-numbers of industrial production except that it is extended to all forms of activity within the production boundary. In practice, when constructing an index-number of industrial production it is usual to assume that an industry's intermediate inputs are proportional to its output, and so the value added in each industry is multiplied by a single indicator of quantity change. Further details on this subject can be found in [37].

5. *Total Product at Constant Prices: Britain*

Let us now return to the *Blue Book* and see how these comparisons work out in practice. Some of them, taken principally from tables 13 and 14 of the *Blue Book* and from [25], are shown in table 9 below. The first two rows of this table show alternative series for the gross domestic product at factor cost recalculated at the values of 1958. We have just seen that in principle these two series should be identical but in practice the data available do not permit a completely integrated calculation. The third row shows the gross domestic product at market prices, and the remaining rows show the composition of this total in terms of the main categories of final product. Here, as is usual, gross domestic product is defined to exclude imports at their cost to Britain; we have not followed the *Blue Book* in deducting also indirect taxes on imports. Consequently, the 1958 figures in this table agree with those in table 1 above.

Although the series in table 9 are expressed at constant prices, the magnitude of the figures makes it difficult to take in at a glance the trends of production. These become more evident if each series is expressed in index-number form with the base year equal to 100. Table 10 below gives all the items of table 9 expressed in this form, with the addition of a subdivision of item 1 by industry. In principle these index-numbers are of Laspeyres' type with 1958 as the base, though some of the components may deviate from this. The figures are again derived from tables 13 and 14 of the *Blue Book* and from [25]. The last column, which shows the ratio of 1964 to 1948, has been added in order to make the comparison between the beginning and the end of the postwar period easier.

We can see from these tables that, after a decade in which normal growth was disrupted by the war, the gross domestic product increased between 1948 and 1964 by 60 per cent, which implies an average annual increase of 3 per cent. This average, however, was not realised every year: between 1954 and 1956 there was a spurt, followed by a pause, followed by another spurt between 1958 and 1960 and then by another pause and another spurt.

If we want to know how the different industries contributed to these changes we can find the answer in the top part of table 10. Rises well above the average took place in public

utilities, in insurance, banking and finance, and in manu-
facturing. Rises around the average took place in agriculture,
construction and distribution. Lowest of all we find mining
and quarrying, which declined during the war and never
regained its prewar level, and public administration and
defence, whose uneven course is mainly due to the fluctuations
of defence expenditure.

From the lower part of the tables we see what happened to
the main categories of final product. Private consumption rose
steadily to a figure 52 per cent above the 1948 level. Public
consumption rose sharply between 1938 and 1954, then fell,
then rose again until in 1964 it was 38 per cent above its 1948
level. The largest increase is that shown by gross investment,
which rose nearly one and a half times between 1948 and 1964.
Exports increased by 85 per cent and imports, which showed a
rather more irregular movement, by 89 per cent. This comparison of exports and imports is perhaps unduly favourable,
however: if we make the comparison with 1958 rather than
1948, we can see that in the last six years exports have risen
by 22 per cent while imports have risen by 36 per cent.

Tables 9 and 10 express quantity changes. If we want to use
them to measure price changes we must divide the entries that
interest us into the corresponding figures at current values. Let
us assume, for instance, that we want to measure the average
price change between 1948 and 1964. We see from table 9
that at 1958 market prices the gross domestic product rose
from £17,760 million to £28,484 million; and if we go back to
table 1, we see that at current market prices it rose during the
same period from £11,730 million to £32,442 million. Accordingly, $(32,442/28,484)/(11,730/17,760) = 1·72$ indicates the
rise in prices between 1948 and 1964 as measured by a Paasche
index-number of prices with $1958 = 100$.

Similarly, if we want to derive this price change from index-
numbers, we must first put the current values for the 1948 and
1964 totals in index-number form, with $1958 = 100$, and then
divide them by the corresponding figures in table 10. Thus at
current prices the gross domestic product rose from 52 in

TABLE 9

Gross Domestic Product Revalued at Constant (1958) Values
United Kingdom

(1958 £ million)

	1938	1948	1954	1957	1958	1959	1960	1961	1962	1963	1964
1. Gross domestic product at factor cost (value added) ..	14,377	16,028	18,940	20,105	20,085	20,989	22,114	22,515	22,796	23,560	24,925
2. Gross domestic product at factor cost (final product)	13,543	15,708	18,791	20,151	20,085	20,803	21,858	22,633	22,796	23,756	24,982
3. Gross domestic product at market prices (final product)	15,773	17,760	21,182	22,682	22,734	23,700	24,904	25,717	25,885	27,037	28,484
(a) Consumers' expenditure											
(i) Private	12,190	12,518	13,991	14,989	15,373	16,089	16,737	17,124	17,461	18,270	18,943
(ii) Public	2,337	3,072	3,954	3,754	3,675	3,751	3,831	3,978	4,100	4,175	4,254
(b) Gross domestic investment											
(i) Fixed assets ..	2,322	2,135	2,982	3,467	3,478	3,751	4,122	4,481	4,443	4,588	5,321
(ii) Stocks	0	250	54	242	100	174	592	319	76	177	482
(c) Exports	2,588	3,113	4,210	4,785	4,707	4,834	5,107	5,252	5,341	5,572	5,746
(d) less Imports ..	-3,664	-3,328	-4,009	-4,555	-4,599	-4,899	-5,485	-5,437	-5,536	-5,745	-6,262

TABLE 10

Index-numbers of Gross Domestic Product at Constant (1958) Values

United Kingdom

(1958 = 100)

	1938	1948	1954	1957	1958	1959	1960	1961	1962	1963	1964	1964 / 1948
1. Gross domestic product at factor cost (value added)												
(a) Agriculture, forestry and fishing	72	80	94	100	100	105	110	112	114	117	124	1·55
(b) Mining and quarrying	70	80	96	102	100	104	111	112	115	119	125	1·56
(c) Manufacturing	114	96	106	104	100	97	94	93	95	95	95	0·99
(d) Construction	60	72	94	101	100	106	115	115	115	120	130	1·81
(e) Gas, electricity and water	95	83	95	101	100	106	111	120	121	121	135	1·63
(f) Transport and communication	39	58	84	96	100	103	110	116	125	133	138	2·38
(g) Distributive trades	65	85	97	101	100	104	110	112	113	117	123	1·45
(h) Insurance, banking and finance	83	76	91	98	100	106	111	112	113	117	122	1·61
(i) Ownership of dwellings	74	75	89	96	100	110	116	120	122	128	134	1·79
(j) Professional and scientific services	81	88	92	98	100	102	104	106	108	110	111	1·26
(k) Miscellaneous services	65	72	88	97	100	103	105	110	114	116	119	1·65
(l) Public administration and defence	123	100	95	98	100	103	108	111	114	117	125	1·25
	71	109	110	104	100	98	97	97	97	99	100	0·92
2. Gross domestic product at factor cost (final product)	68	78	94	100	100	104	109	113	114	118	124	1·59
3. Gross domestic product at market prices (final product)	70	78	93	100	100	104	110	113	114	119	125	1·60
(a) Consumers' expenditure												
(i) Private	80	81	91	97	100	105	109	111	114	119	123	1·52
(ii) Public	63	84	108	102	100	102	104	108	112	114	116	1·38
(b) Gross domestic investment*	65	67	85	104	100	110	132	134	126	133	162	2·42
(c) Exports	55	66	89	102	100	103	108	112	113	118	122	1·85
(d) Imports	80	72	87	99	100	107	119	118	120	125	136	1·89

* Includes investment in stocks. For fixed assets alone the series was: 67, 61, 86, 100, 100, 108, 119, 129, 128, 132, 153; 153/61 = 2·51.

1948 to 100 in 1958 and 143 in 1964; at 1958 prices the corresponding figures were 78, 100 and 125. The implicit price series is therefore $52/78 = 0·67$, $100/100 = 1$ and $143/125 = 1·14$. And $1·14/0·67 = 1·70$, which, allowing for rounding-off errors, is the same percentage as we reached above.

By now the point of these calculations should be clear. Table 1 tells us that between 1948 and 1964 the gross domestic product increased in money terms by 177 per cent. By making index-numbers of quantities and prices we see that in real terms it rose in fact by about 60 per cent and that the rest of the increase was only apparent, being due to a rise of about 72 per cent in prices. This is a big step forward in our analysis of economic events, though we must always remember that if we had reversed the roles of Laspeyres and Paasche or had chosen the relative values of a different year our answers would have been slightly different.

6. *Total Product at Constant Prices: America*

The course of the real product totals in America is set out in table 11 below. The estimates are based on table 2 of the *Survey*, with adjustments made with the help of information not available in the *Survey*. These adjustments are necessary because the Americans record only national, and not domestic, totals and restrict investment to private investment (although they do make separate estimates of government expenditure on structures).

The first thing we see from table 11 is the great increase in American productive activity over the war period: between 1938 and 1948 their gross domestic product rose by 68 per cent (or 5·2 per cent per annum) as opposed to 13 per cent (or 1·2 per cent per annum) in Britain. After the war the rate of growth, though still faster than in Britain, slowed down somewhat: over the sixteen years between 1948 and 1964 the total increase was 78 per cent (or 3·6 per cent per annum).

The components of the gross domestic product too followed a very different course from that of their British counterparts:

TABLE 11

Gross Domestic Product at Constant (1958) Values
United States

(1958 $ milliard; 1958 = 100)

	1938	1948	1954	1957	1958	1959	1960	1961	1962	1963	1964
1. Gross domestic product at market prices	191·8	322·5	405·2	450·4	445·2	473·6	485·4	494·2	526·5	546·7	573·6
(a) Consumers' expenditure											
(i) Private	140·2	210·8	255·7	288·2	290·1	307·3	316·2	322·6	338·6	352·4	372·1
(ii) Public	27·5	40·4	75·7	75·1	78·5	78·6	79·2	83·6	90·4	92·3	92·7
(b) Gross domestic investment											
(i) Fixed assets	25·8	61·8	74·6	81·8	78·1	84·9	84·6	83·9	90·5	94·1	99·7
(ii) Stocks	-2·4	4·6	-2·0	1·2	-1·5	4·8	3·5	2·0	6·0	5·7	4·6
(c) Exports	8·3	16·6	16·6	23·4	20·2	20·7	23·9	24·1	25·5	27·5	31·1
(d) less Imports	-7·6	-11·7	-15·4	-19·3	-20·2	-22·7	-22·0	-22·0	-24·5	-25·3	-26·6
2. Index numbers of gross domestic product at market prices	43	72	91	101	100	106	109	111	118	123	129
(a) Consumers' expenditure											
(i) Private	48	73	88	99	100	106	109	111	117	121	128
(ii) Public	35	51	96	96	100	100	101	106	115	118	118
(b) Gross domestic investment*	31	87	95	108	100	117	115	112	126	130	136
(c) Exports	41	82	82	116	100	102	118	119	126	136	154
(d) Imports	38	58	76	96	100	112	109	109	121	125	132

* Includes investment in stocks. For fixed assets alone the series was: 33, 79, 96, 105, 100, 108, 107, 116, 120, 128.

between 1948 and 1964, private consumption rose by 77 per cent; public consumption by 129 per cent; investment in fixed assets by 61 per cent; exports by 87 per cent; and imports by 127 per cent. Thus while in Britain consumption rose rather more slowly and investment much faster than product, in America the position was reversed, which at first sight would suggest a rather happy-go-lucky attitude towards investment.

Before we jump to any such conclusion, however, we shall be wise to go back to what we said on p. 33 about investment as a percentage of total product. From tables 9 and 11 we see that at constant prices the ratio of fixed investment to gross domestic product in 1938 was nearly 15 per cent in Britain and over 13 per cent in America; in 1948 it was 12 per cent in Britain and 19 per cent in America; and in 1964 it was nearly 19 per cent in Britain and over 17 per cent in America. This puts the course of events in better perspective: America, less strained by the war, had reached by 1948 a high ratio of investment to product, which dropped only slightly in recent years; in Britain this ratio in 1948 was still relatively low, and it was only in the 1960's that it managed to catch up with the American percentage and eventually overtake it.

Another point to bear in mind is that in all the comparisons we have made so far we have only discussed the growth of the two economies as collective units and have not considered how this growth affected the individuals within these units. For this purpose the first thing to do is to put these comparisons on a per head basis. Between 1948 and 1964 the gross domestic product of Britain rose by 60 per cent, that of America by 78 per cent; at the same time the population of Britain increased from 49·6 to 54·2 million, that of America from 147·2 to 192·1 million. Thus the gross domestic product *per head of the population* rose by 47 per cent (or 2·4 per cent per annum) in Britain and 36 per cent (or 1·9 per cent per annum) in America.

As usual, however, this first conclusion, though correct in a sense and quite useful, is too simple. What does 'per head' mean? The large increase in the American population consists partly of an increase in the proportion of babies and young children, who do not consume so much product as adults do: if more cars are produced, this does not mean that the new generations of Americans go to their kindergarden driving their Cadillacs, but that their parents can now afford two cars instead of one. To pursue these calculations to a great degree of refinement is impossible without investigating the age distribution of the population and the relative capacity for consumption of the different age groups. In this short book we shall not go into these matters. We have only mentioned them here as another example of how careful one has to be in order to make valid comparisons.

7. Quarterly Series

As we said at the end of Chapter I, nowadays both Britain and America produce a large number of quarterly statistics which enable the national accounts to be kept up to date. For Britain the quarterly series appear in the October, January, April and July numbers of Economic Trends [33] and are keyed in to the annual estimates given in September of each year in the Blue Book. These series go back to 1955 and cover most aspects of the national accounts, though in much less detail than the Blue Book does; in particular, there are no quarterly figures for depreciation, so that the estimates of income, product, saving and investment exist only on a gross basis. Although most of the series are expressed only at current values, those for final product and its main components are also expressed at constant values.

Similar information for America can be found in the Survey.

When one passes from annual to quarterly series a new difficulty arises in making valid comparisons: quarterly series are, to a greater or less extent, subject to seasonal influences which obscure their underlying trend. This is not the place in which to embark on a lengthy description of the problems of seasonal adjustment; a discussion of many of the issues, both conceptual and practical, can be found in [22,27]. Nevertheless a few words on the subject, in addition to what was said in section 3 above, may be useful.

If we draw a graph of a quarterly (or monthly) economic series, we usually find that it exhibits visible fluctuations from season to season, which more or less repeat themselves year after year. For example, if we take consumers' expenditure in Britain we find that as a rule it is about 6 per cent below trend during the first quarter, about 1 per cent above trend during the second and third quarters and about 5 per cent above trend during the last quarter. Such variations, which of course differ greatly from one series to another, are due to a large number of causes: climatic conditions, such as temperature, rainfall and sunshine; the vagaries of the calendar, such as the incidence of normal working days and moveable feasts; and human responses to these factors, such as the fixing of holiday periods and the discontinuities that arise in production from, say, the difference between summer and winter clothing. Some of these factors are constant and produce constant seasonal patterns: Christmas comes at the same time every year and with it the demand for turkeys and small fir trees soars. Some change gradually and the patterns change gradually with them: as more and more employers grant holidays with pay, more and more people take summer holidays and more and more establishments have to close down during that season. Finally, some are irregular and produce irregularities in the patterns: a late warm Easter will send record crowds to the seaside; a very cold winter will lead to an abnormally high consumption of fuel.

With so many influences at work some kind of strategy is needed in approaching the problem of seasonal adjustment. In the first place, although most economic series follow a seasonal pattern, it should not be too readily assumed that all do, since not all variations have seasonal causes: wars, changes of government, movements of population, fashions are not seasonal phenomena, yet they too may produce noticeable peaks and troughs in a series. The first step, therefore, is to try to decide whether the variations in a series are due to seasonal influences or not.

For this purpose we need not consider seasonal factors; the

clue lies in the pattern formed by the observations themselves. In order to find out what this pattern is like, we must first fit a trend to the series as a whole, so that the observations can be expressed as deviations from the trend; if we then group these deviations by season and calculate each season's average, we can see (i) what the position of the individual observations is in relation to their respective averages and (ii) what the position of the averages is in relation to each other. If the observations are widely dispersed around their averages and if at the same time the averages lie fairly close together, we shall know that the seasonal averages cannot be determined accurately (unless the series is a very long one) and that anyway seasonal factors account for only a small proportion of the total variation. Little would be gained, therefore, from seasonal adjustment; indeed, if the dispersion of the averages, that is their distance from each other, is sufficiently small in relation to the dispersion of the observations around them, it could well happen that in the future the averages would change their respective positions, with the result that the seasonal pattern we had observed in the past would be positively misleading for the future. If on the other hand both the dispersion of the observations and the dispersion of the averages are wide, we shall know that seasonal factors do play a definite part in the total variation, even though the determination of the averages may not be very accurate; alternatively, if both dispersions are small we shall know not only that the variations are mainly due to seasonal factors but also that the averages are likely to be pretty accurate. In either case a seasonal adjustment would be appropriate.

Having decided that an adjustment is required, the next step is to consider how to carry it out. This depends on whether the seasonal pattern we have found is constant or shows signs of gradual change from year to year. In the first case we can eliminate the seasonal variations by removing from each observation the relevant seasonal average, or seasonal constant. In the second case we must replace these constants by variables which change gradually with time. These variables, however,

TAB

Quarterly Series of Gross Domestic Pr
Un

(19

	1962			
	i	ii	iii	
Gross domestic product at market prices (final product)	**6,197**	**6,555**	**6,457**	**6,**
(a) Consumers' expenditure				
(i) Private	4,086	4,406	4,365	4,
(ii) Public	1,025	1,020	1,022	1,
(b) Gross domestic investment				
(i) Fixed assets	1,123	1,081	1,107	1,
(ii) Stocks	17	54	78	
(c) Exports	1,299	1,380	1,313	1,
(d) less Imports	−1,353	−1,386	−1,428	−1,

TAB

Quarterly Series of Gross Domestic Pr
Un

(19

	1962			
	i	ii	iii	
Gross domestic product at market prices (final product)	**6,373**	**6,517**	**6,502**	**6,**
(a) Consumers' expenditure				
(i) Private	4,310	4,357	4,357	4,
(ii) Public	1,017	1,023	1,025	1,
(b) Gross domestic investment				
(i) Fixed assets	1,101	1,125	1,124	1,
(ii) Stocks	−9	35	70	
(c) Exports	1,310	1,352	1,337	1,
(d) less Imports	−1,356	−1,375	−1,411	−1,

Constant (1958) Values, Unadjusted
gdom

on)

	1963			1964				1965	
	ii	iii	iv	i	ii	iii	iv	i	ii
3	**6,821**	**6,713**	**7,190**	**6,842**	**7,169**	**7,044**	**7,429**	**7,087**	**7,267**
9	4,608	4,637	4,806	4,476	4,761	4,758	4,948	4,609	4,796
6	1,041	1,037	1,051	1,064	1,055	1,063	1,072	1,074	1,107
1	1,100	1,178	1,279	1,299	1,266	1,326	1,430	1,398	1,320
9	82	−1	87	105	188	119	70	81	105
4	1,419	1,363	1,426	1,427	1,478	1,381	1,460	1,424	1,521
6	−1,429	−1,501	−1,459	−1,529	−1,579	−1,603	−1,551	−1,499	−1,582

Constant (1958) Values, Seasonally Adjusted
gdom

ion)

	1963			1964				1965	
	ii	iii	iv	i	ii	iii	iv	i	ii
3	**6,786**	**6,774**	**6,994**	**7,025**	**7,095**	**7,115**	**7,249**	**7,335**	**7,171**
9	4,546	4,623	4,652	4,726	4,690	4,730	4,797	4,877	4,722
8	1,044	1,040	1,053	1,055	1,057	1,066	1,076	1,067	1,109
7	1,155	1,194	1,232	1,266	1,323	1,348	1,384	1,378	1,379
7	70	3	121	87	164	123	108	56	85
6	1,390	1,387	1,419	1,436	1,433	1,421	1,456	1,473	1,450
0	−1,419	−1,473	−1,483	−1,545	−1,572	−1,573	−1,572	−1,516	−1,574

must be regularly re-examined, since even small monotonic movements will produce in time a substantial alteration in the seasonal pattern and cannot therefore be expected to persist for long with undiminished vigour. This method, which is an application of the analysis of variance and covariance, is explained in detail and exemplified in [27].

So far we have tried, more or less mechanically, to associate with each season a regular deviation, either constant or slowly changing, from the trend, without considering what factors lie behind these deviations. The third step is to examine such factors and see how far they may account for irregularities in the pattern. For example, a normal pattern shows a higher consumption of fuel in winter than in summer; we know that this is due to temperature; so we may legitimately conclude that if one winter the consumption of fuel was abnormally high this was most probably due to an abnormally cold season. This may seem painfully obvious. But the fact is that in tracing such connections a good deal of care is needed, for various reasons. Thus abnormality in a given factor may not have consistent effects in all seasons: an abnormally cold winter will indeed lead to an abnormally high consumption of fuel, but an abnormally hot summer cannot lead to an abnormally low consumption of fuel if no fuel is used for heating in normal summers; on the contrary, if a substantial number of the buildings in a country are air-conditioned, an abnormally hot summer will lead to an abnormally high consumption of fuel for cooling. Also, different factors, such as temperature and sunshine, are correlated, so that their effects may be hard to disentangle. Because of these and other pitfalls the third step, finding the causes of seasonal irregularities, is much the most laborious and not unnaturally statisticians tend very often to stop short of it.

However far we go in attempting to adjust a series for seasonal variations, the object is the same: to get a better estimate of the underlying movements of the series, undisturbed by purely seasonal factors. Examples of quarterly series before and after adjustment are given in tables 12 and 13. These tables, which are derived from the October 1965 issue of *Economic Trends*, show the quarterly course of the gross domestic product and its main components in Britain from the beginning of 1962 to the middle of 1965, and are directly comparable with the lower part of table 9: for each series, the sum of the four quarters in each year in either table is equal to the total for that year given in table 9. Similar tables could be compiled for America from the *Survey*; but they would not be fully comparable with the annual figures given in table 11 because American quarterly information on foreign transactions is not detailed enough to enable us to separate imports and exports from factor incomes paid abroad and received from abroad.

The contrast between adjusted and unadjusted quarterly movements, and between these and annual movements, can be seen more clearly still in diagram 2. This diagram is constructed partly from table 9 and partly from tables 12 and 13. Each series starts in 1957 and ends in 1965. The period 1957–61 is shown as an annual run, the period 1962–5 as a twofold quarterly run, the dotted lines indicating the pattern formed by the actual observations, the solid lines the pattern that emerges after seasonal adjustment. The points representing the annual figures have been brought down to a quarterly level by dividing each year's total by four. Visually, these points are placed in mid-year, while those representing the quarterly figures are placed in mid-quarter; hence the gap between 1961 and the first quarter of 1962. The scales for the individual series alternate between left and right; thus the scale for imports, which goes from £1,100 million to £1,600 million, is the lowest on the left; that for exports, which goes from £1,100 million to £1,500 million, is the next up on the right; that for investment in fixed assets, which goes from £900 million to £1,400 million, is again on the left; and so on. Product levels are measured on a logarithmic or ratio scale, which means that a given vertical distance represents a given proportionate difference and not a given absolute one; thus the distance separating 900 from 1,000 is the same as that separating 4,500 from 5,000. On this

DIAGRAM 2
Gross Domestic Product and its Components
United Kingdom (*1958 £ million*)

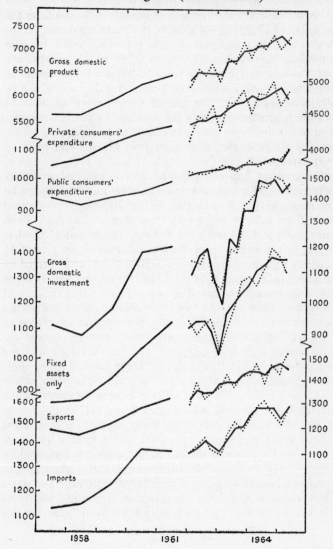

scale an upward-sloping line corresponds to a constant proportionate rate of growth over time.

One point which becomes very evident from this diagram is the different sensitivity of the different series to seasonal influences. Private consumers' expenditure has very marked and regular deviations: it is always at its highest in the fourth quarter and at its lowest in the first. Public expenditure, on the other hand, deviates very little from the trend at any season. Investment in fixed assets is always above average in the first quarter and below average in the second; this is visible even in the abnormally deep trough at the beginning of 1963. Whatever their underlying trend, exports tend always to drop and imports always to rise in the third quarter. Not surprisingly, gross domestic product as a whole has a pattern rather similar to that of its biggest constituent, private consumers' expenditure.

CHAPTER IV

COMPARISONS OVER SPACE

1. *Britain and America Compared: Levels*

IN CHAPTER III we have seen how comparisons over time can be made in terms of a given set of relative values. We shall now see that exactly the same technique can be applied to comparisons over space. When we were considering index-number formulae in section 2 of the last chapter we identified the symbols 0 and 1 with two different periods. We might equally well have identified them with two different countries, and so built an index-number bridge across space instead of building it across time.

Let us take two countries, Britain and America. For each of them let us make a list of all the commodities which constitute final product. Now, assuming that Britain $= 0$ and America $= 1$, we can draw up a set of quantity ratios, q_1/q_0, which will show the quantity level of each commodity in America as a proportion of its quantity level in Britain. If we now multiply each of these ratios by the corresponding expenditure in Britain and add up the resulting values thus, $\Sigma[p_0q_0(q_1/q_0)]$, we shall have a measure of American final product valued at British prices. If we divide this by total expenditure in Britain, Σp_0q_0, we shall get Laspeyres' index-number of quantities, $\Sigma p_0q_1/\Sigma p_0q_0$, which compares the levels of final product in the two countries in terms of British relative prices. In a similar way we can calculate the corresponding Paasche quantity index, $\Sigma p_1q_1/\Sigma p_1q_0$, which compares them in terms of American prices.

Having determined the quantity indices, we can then obtain price indices by dividing the ratio of actual expenditures in the two countries, $\Sigma p_1q_1/\Sigma p_0q_0$, by either of the quantity indices. If we use Laspeyres' quantity index as the divisor we shall obtain Paasche's price index, $\Sigma p_1 q_1 / \Sigma p_0 q_1$, which will relate two valuations of American final product, one expressed in dollars, the other in pounds. If on the other hand we use Paasche's quantity index as the divisor we shall obtain Laspeyres' price index, $\Sigma p_1 q_0 / \Sigma p_0 q_0$, which will show us the relationship between the dollar and the pound valuations of British final product. By either operation we shall get a measure of the average purchasing power of the dollar in relation to the average purchasing power of the pound. As we have seen in the last chapter, however, the conclusions reached through Laspeyres' method may not tally with those reached through Paasche's, and in such cases the best answer devised so far is Fisher's ideal index, which is the geometric average of the other two.

On the whole, comparisons over space are more difficult to make and quantitatively less certain than comparisons over time, by which we mean reasonably short time-spans, say a generation. The reasons for this are: first, that relative values tend to differ more between countries than between two not very distant periods in the same country; second, that the individual commodities used to satisfy the same wants in different countries are often different and thus not easy to compare; and third, that the information available is also different in different countries, depending very much on the degree of development of the various statistical services and on the categories and classifications which they employ.

The most thorough analysis of comparative national products and price levels so far available has been published by the O.E.E.C. in [12]. This study contains a detailed comparison between the United States and eight European countries, Britain, Belgium, Denmark, France, Germany, Italy, the Netherlands and Norway, in 1950 and 1955. America is treated as the base and each European country is compared with it first in terms of American relative prices and then in terms of its own prices. For certain purposes use is also made of a set of 'average European prices'. We shall see the point of this concept in section 3 below.

According to the O.E.E.C. study, in 1950 the British gross national product *per head of the population* was 62 per cent of the American in terms of American relative prices but only 48 per cent in terms of British prices. The corresponding percentages for 1955 are 64 and 50. These quantity indices are respectively Laspeyres' and Paasche's with America treated as the base. The difference is considerable in both years, showing to what extent this kind of comparison is affected by the values chosen as weights, but we should not be disconcerted by it; after all, the two pairs of index-numbers do give us an idea of the range in which to place the British standard of living in respect to the American, and if we want to express its position by a single figure for each year we can take Fisher's index-numbers, which are 54 per cent in 1950 and 56 per cent in 1955.

The figures given in [12] refer to final product. There is however an alternative approach to international comparisons just as there is to comparisons over time, namely value added. This approach has been explored by Paige and Bombach in their comparison between Britain and America in [24]. While in principle the two approaches should lead to identical results, in this case the calculations done on value added were somewhat more favourable to Britain, suggesting that those done on final product overestimate the difference between the two countries.

But why, it may be asked, go to all this trouble to calculate the relative economic positions of Britain and America when we could simply compare totals through the official rate of exchange? The answer is that if we chose this apparently straightforward approach, the exchange rate, approximately £1 = $2·8, would place Britain at 37 per cent of the American level in 1950 and 42 per cent in 1955, which shows that despite the range of uncertainty of the index-number calculations the figures yielded by the exchange rate lie well outside that range and exaggerate the difference between the two countries. This confirms the common belief that since the devaluation of 1949 the internal purchasing power of the pound has been officially undervalued in relation to that of the dollar. We shall see in the next section that in 1938 the position was reversed and it was the dollar that was undervalued in relation to the pound. The conclusion is that exchange rates, though temptingly simple, are a most unreliable guide and should as far as possible be avoided when making international comparisons.

2. Britain and America Compared: Levels and Trends

Tables 9 and 11 of the preceding chapter showed the course of the gross domestic product in Britain and America since 1938. In order to carry the comparison further back it is more convenient, however, to use national product totals. Annual estimates of the gross national product at constant prices are available in both countries for the last sixty years; if we divide them year by year by the number of inhabitants and express the results in one currency we shall obtain two comparable series which will show the course of real product per head in each country. This is done for 1909–64, using the pound as the currency unit, in table 14 below. The two war periods are omitted because the data, especially for Britain, are either unreliable or altogether missing.

TABLE 14

Gross National Product per Head of the Population, 1909–1964
United Kingdom and United States

(1955 £)

	1909	1910	1911	1912	1913	1914 1919	1920	1921	1922	1923	1924	1925	1926	1927	1928
U.K.	259	266	271	272	279	...	265	240	240	247	253	269	253	272	277
U.S.	329	331	334	349	344	...	338	303	346	382	374	400	416	410	408
	1929	1930	1931	1932	1933	1934	1935	1936	1937	1938	1939 1945	1946	1947	1948	1949
U.K.	283	279	257	254	255	277	286	294	307	305	...	325	312	323	330
U.S.	430	383	351	297	290	314	343	388	406	383	...	567	552	566	557
	1950	1951	1952	1953	1954	1955	1956	1957	1958	1959	1960	1961	1962	1963	1964
U.K.	343	352	348	362	374	383	389	395	395	408	425	425	433	451	470
U.S.	599	638	646	664	643	680	680	678	659	690	695	697	731	748	775

The two series in this table are linked together at one point, 1955, the course of each being determined by a comparison over time in each country. The exchange rate implied is £1 = $3·4, which is the geometric average of the two price ratios yielded by Paasche's and Laspeyres' price indices for 1955.

As to the sources of the figures, the series for Britain is derived up to 1937 from the estimates given by Feinstein in [25], as follows: the current-price totals of gross national product are divided by the implicit price index, 1958 = 100, based on the gross domestic product at market prices; and the resulting constant-price totals are then divided by the population as given elsewhere in [25]. From 1938 onwards the figures are derived in the same way from the *Blue Book*. The whole series is then converted from 1958 to 1955 prices by multiplying it through by a constant so as to bring the gross national product per head in 1955 in line with the O.E.E.C. figure for Britain in [12]. In contrast with the estimates given in former editions of this book, the whole series, and not merely the figures from 1938 onwards, is based on statistics of expenditure rather than of income. It is mainly for this reason that the figures for the earlier years, up to the great depression of the 1930's, are a little higher than those given formerly.

The series for America is also derived from two sources, [51] and the *Survey*. The former gives estimates of the gross national product from 1909 to 1928 at 1954 prices, the latter gives them from 1929 to 1964 at 1958 prices. These two sets of estimates are linked together to form a continuous series, which is then, as in the case of Britain, divided by the population and finally multiplied through by a constant so that the figure for 1955 should equal the O.E.E.C. figure for America.

Table 14 makes it possible to compare the levels of product in Britain and America year by year but not to take in at a glance either their movements over time or their changing relationship to each other. All this becomes clear if the figures are represented graphically, as in diagram 3 below.

DIAGRAM 3

Gross National Product per Head of the Population,
1909–1964. United Kingdom and United States

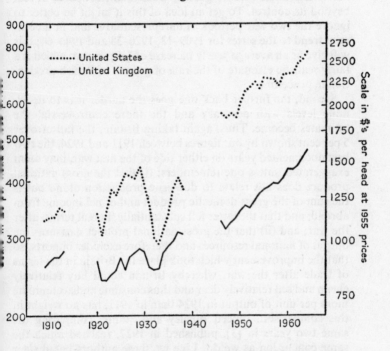

This diagram is provided with two units of measurement,
1955 pounds and 1955 dollars. As in the case of diagram 2,
product levels are measured on a logarithmic scale, which
means that an upward-sloping straight line corresponds to a
constant proportionate rate of growth over time.

In studying diagram 3 the following comments may be useful.
First, the disrupting effects of the two world wars make it
difficult to summarize the growth of real product per head in

either country in terms of simple trends. If we take Britain and draw a straight line from 1909 to 1964 we obtain an average annual rate of growth of 1·1 per cent, which is a measure of the country's performance over the fifty-five years but gives no indication of its rate of growth when undisturbed by forces beyond its control. To get an idea of this it might be better to ignore the two war periods as unrepresentative and fit a common trend to the series for 1909–13, 1920–38 and 1946–64; this will give us an average yearly increase of 1·6 per cent, which is a fairly realistic estimate of the rate of growth of British production in peacetime.

Second, the further back one goes the harder it is to determine levels with accuracy and the more controversial the estimates become. Thus, again taking Britain, the fall of over 5 per cent shown by our figures between 1911 and 1924, the two best documented years on either side of the first war, may seem exaggerated unless one remembers: (i) that the gross national product does not relate to domestic production alone but is the sum of the gross domestic product and of net income from abroad, and that the latter fell substantially, in real terms, after the war; and (ii) that the gross national product measures the output of national resources and therefore excludes imports, so that the improvement which took place for Britain in the terms of trade after the war, whereby Britain could buy relatively cheap and sell relatively dear and thus consume and accumulate more per unit of output in 1924 than in 1911, has no weight in this comparison. Indeed Bowley and Stamp, comparing the same two years in [3], published in 1927, reached much the same conclusion as we do. Like us, these authors based their calculations on money values and price movements and it is interesting to note that to them, far from appearing pessimistic, a fall of 5 per cent between 1911 and 1924 appeared surprisingly small when compared with the production statistics then available; we know now, from the recent researches of Lomax [18] and others, that these statistics considerably underestimated the rise in production during the first quarter of the century.

Third, when we turn to America matters are further complicated by the great depression of the thirties. If we follow the line of thought suggested above and, ignoring the two wars, fit a common trend to the three peacetime series, we get an average yearly rate of growth of 0·9 per cent, which seems unduly low. Perhaps it would be fairer to regard the whole of the inter-war period as a piece of misfortune which is unlikely to recur, as much an act of God as a war, and calculate the country's normal rate of growth from the experience of 1909–13 and 1946–64, in which case it works out at 1·5 per cent per annum.

Fourth, when we compare the two countries we see that the American series has been above the British throughout, but in a most uneven manner. Thus, immediately before the first war it was about one-fourth higher; by 1924 the difference had increased to 50 per cent, only to fall to 14 per cent in 1933; in 1938 it had increased again to about 26 per cent. The second war, by turning America into an arsenal, absorbed all the labour unemployed in the thirties and gave an abnormal stimulus to production, with the result that in 1946 the difference between the two countries increased to about 75 per cent; by 1955, this difference was about 78 per cent, but by 1964 it had been reduced to 65 per cent. This last figure may be compared with the crude calculations made on p. 24 above.

Finally, it is interesting to compare the price ratios of the two countries with the course of the exchange rate between the dollar and the pound. This is done for selected years in table 15 below.

The falling series in the first column shows simply that prices have been rising faster in Britain than in America, with the consequence that through time the pound has come to buy less and less in comparison with the dollar. The series in the second column shows the course of the exchange rate. In spite of the fact that the two series move in the same general direction, a glance at the figures brings out once again the danger of using exchange rates for the purpose of international comparisons. This is recognized when exchange rates are fixed officially but

TABLE 15

Dollar-Pound Equivalents, 1913–1964

	Price ratios linked in 1955	Exchange rates
1913 ..	5·3	4·9
1924 ..	4·6	4·4
1938 ..	4·1	4·9
1950 ..	3·8	2·8
1955 ..	3·4	2·8
1960 ..	3·3	2·8
1964 ..	3·1	2·8

may apply quite as strongly when they are not. Even under free market conditions it is not to be expected that they will exactly reflect the ratio of internal prices: there may be political reasons why a particular currency is either specially sought after or mistrusted abroad, or the products exported by a country may be highly specialized, so that the national price level will be unrepresentative of their price level on the international market. Thus we see that the pound from being undervalued in 1913 got even in 1924 and became considerably overvalued between 1924 and 1938, owing partly to the political unrest of continental Europe and partly perhaps to the American depression; the position was reversed in the devaluation of 1949, thereby giving Britain some export advantage over America; but the persistently higher rate of increase in British prices has much reduced this advantage and is bringing the two series together again. If we had compared Britain and America in 1924 on the basis of the exchange rate we should not have gone seriously wrong, but in 1938 we should have over-estimated the British national product by about one-fifth, and underestimated it by about one-fifth in 1955.

It is important not to claim too much for the kind of comparison made in this section: we have seen something of the theoretical difficulties involved and these are increased by the incompleteness of the available statistics, especially for the more distant past. But it is even more important not to adopt a nihilistic attitude to such comparisons: if carefully done, they provide the best guide we have to relative levels and trends and are our only means of judging performance and achievement in different parts of the world.

3. *Rings and Chains of Comparisons*

Before we go on to the other European countries included in the O.E.E.C. study, let us digress for a moment on the comparison of three or more situations, whether in space or in time. Suppose we have three countries, or three periods, distinguished by the suffixes 0, 1 and 2. If we compared first 0 with 1, then 1 with 2 and finally 2 with 0 we might hope to end up with the same value for 0 that we started from; in other words, the product of the binary comparisons round the ring should multiply out to 1. We can be certain that this result will follow identically only if the same set of relative values is used for all the comparisons, though in freak cases it may follow by chance even if this condition is not satisfied.

This statement can be verified by extending the formulae given in section 2 of Chapter III above. If we go round the ring of comparisons using Laspeyres' quantity index for each link we obtain

$$\frac{\Sigma p_0 q_1}{\Sigma p_0 q_0} \cdot \frac{\Sigma p_1 q_2}{\Sigma p_1 q_1} \cdot \frac{\Sigma p_2 q_0}{\Sigma p_2 q_2} \neq 1 \qquad \ldots (9)$$

because in general the terms of the product do not cancel out. Thus the ring is not properly closed. If we now try using Fisher's ideal index-number we obtain

$$\sqrt{\frac{\Sigma p_0 q_1}{\Sigma p_0 q_0} \cdot \frac{\Sigma p_1 q_1}{\Sigma p_1 q_0}} \cdot \sqrt{\frac{\Sigma p_1 q_2}{\Sigma p_1 q_1} \cdot \frac{\Sigma p_2 q_2}{\Sigma p_2 q_1}} \cdot \sqrt{\frac{\Sigma p_2 q_0}{\Sigma p_2 q_2} \cdot \frac{\Sigma p_0 q_0}{\Sigma p_0 q_2}}$$

$$= \sqrt{\frac{\Sigma p_0 q_1}{\Sigma p_0 q_2} \cdot \frac{\Sigma p_1 q_2}{\Sigma p_1 q_0} \cdot \frac{\Sigma p_2 q_0}{\Sigma p_2 q_1}} \neq 1 \qquad \ldots (10)$$

in general, and again the ring is not closed. It will be noticed that in this case each of the three binary comparisons is based on the values of the third country. If more than three countries are compared, the ideal index-number ring, after the cancellation of common terms, has an appearance even more surprising than (10).

The position is different if we choose a common set of relative values for all the comparisons. Let p_c denote prices, c being the country whose values we choose. Then clearly

$$\frac{\Sigma p_c q_1}{\Sigma p_c q_0} \cdot \frac{\Sigma p_c q_2}{\Sigma p_c q_1} \cdot \frac{\Sigma p_c q_0}{\Sigma p_c q_2} = 1 \qquad \ldots (11)$$

identically, since each of the three distinct terms appears in both the numerator and the denominator of this expression. From the point of view of consistency it does not matter what set of relative values is used provided it is the same in each comparison: c may equal 0, 1, 2 or a fourth country outside the comparison, or an average of all or any of these. From the point of view of relevance, however, we must be careful of how we choose c, since if we choose a country whose relative values are very different from those of the countries under comparison we may get a misleading answer.

We can now see the point of the concept of average European prices mentioned in section 1 above. Each direct comparison of a European country with America gives us the best comparison we can make of that country with America, but for intra-European comparisons there is no reason why we should bring American values into the picture; nor is there any reason why we should select the values of any one European country in preference to those of any other. By establishing a set of average European values we get round the difficulty and can compare the eight European countries covered in [12] on a basis which though not ideal will be consistent and fairly relevant. This is done in the form of a ready reckoner in table 16 below. The percentages refer to real product per head.

TABLE 16

Relative Gross National Products per Head in 1955

(1955 Average European Prices)

	United Kingdom	Norway	Belgium	Denmark	Germany	France	Nether-lands	Italy
United Kingdom	1·00	1·02	1·04	1·11	1·15	1·17	1·22	2·12
Norway... ...	0·98	1·00	1·03	1·09	1·13	1·15	1·20	2·09
Belgium ...	0·96	0·98	1·00	1·06	1·10	1·12	1·17	2·03
Denmark ...	0·90	0·92	0·94	1·00	1·04	1·06	1·10	1·91
Germany ...	0·87	0·88	0·91	0·96	1·00	1·02	1·06	1·84
France	0·85	0·87	0·89	0·95	0·98	1·00	1·04	1·81
Netherlands ...	0·82	0·83	0·86	0·91	0·94	0·96	1·00	1·74
Italy	0·47	0·48	0·49	0·52	0·54	0·55	0·57	1·00

Reading this table horizontally, each row gives the country named at its side as a percentage of the countries named at the head of the columns; thus the row for Denmark shows that in 1955 the Danish gross national product per head was 90 per cent of the British and 106 per cent of the French. Reading the table vertically, each column gives all the countries listed down the side as percentages of that named at its head; thus the column for Denmark shows that the British and the French national products were respectively 111 per cent and 95 per cent of the Danish. The consistency of the comparisons is easily checked; for example, if we form the product of the comparisons of France with Britain, Denmark with France, the Netherlands with Denmark, and Italy with the Netherlands we shall reach, apart from rounding-off errors, the same figure as appears in the direct comparison of Italy with Britain: $0·85 \times 1·06 \times 0·91 \times 0·57 = 0·47$.

If, however, we want to obtain a consistent comparison and at the same time follow as closely as possible the individual price and quantity structures of each of the countries concerned, then we must adopt a more sophisticated method than that used by the O.E.E.C. Such a method has been developed and illustrated by van Ijzeren in [15] and a simple form of solution has been suggested by Geary in [11].

4. Europe and America Compared:
the Composition of Gross National Product

In this section we shall compare final product in America with final product in Europe as represented by all the member countries of the O.E.E.C. In [12] each of the eight countries so far considered is compared with America both on the basis of American prices and on that of average European prices, and to complete the picture rough estimates are also given for the remaining member countries, namely Austria, Greece, Iceland, Ireland, Luxembourg, Portugal, Sweden, Switzerland and Turkey, as a group. The results of these comparisons are then summed up in a set of geometric averages which are reproduced in table 17 below. The unit of currency used is the dollar. The definitions of the main components of final product are similar to those used throughout this book but there are certain differences; of these the most important is that all expenditure on health and education is included in private consumption, so that government consumption is restricted to general administration and defence.

Quite a lot can be learnt from this table. In the first place, by studying the figures as they are we can get an idea of the productiveness of the different countries and of the size of the markets for each category of product. For instance, if we compare the first two columns we see that in 1955 the O.E.E.C. countries as a whole produced 27 per cent less than America did, although their combined population exceeded that of America by 73 per cent, and that despite their much greater number the Europeans consumed very little more food than was consumed in America and spent on durables only about one-quarter of what the Americans did.

In the second place, by dividing the items in each column by the respective population figures (row 6) we can assess the actual money value of product and expenditure per head in the different countries and form a fairly concrete estimate of the different standards of living. For instance, total production per head was $2,293 in America, $1,300 in Britain, $1,154 in

TABLE 17

Comparative Gross National Products by Major Categories in 1955

(Money Values in $ milliard and Population in million)

	United States	O.E.E.C. member countries	8 countries combined	United Kingdom	Norway	Belgium	Denmark	Germany	France	Netherlands	Italy	Other O.E.E.C. member countries
1. Gross national product*	377·2	274·1	235·5	66·3	4·3	10·8	5·1	57·6	48·6	11·4	31·5	38·6
2. Private consumption (including health and education)	250·3	185·0	157·7	45·9	2·8	6·9	3·6	36·7	33·8	7·0	21·0	27·3
(a) Food	62·7	68·8	57·8	14·6	0·9	2·5	1·2	14·3	12·3	2·8	9·3	11·0
(b) Clothing	26·1	18·0	15·2	4·0	0·4	0·9	0·4	3·4	3·1	0·9	2·0	2·9
(c) Housing	16·0	13·2	11·3	4·0	0·2	0·4	0·3	2·6	2·2	0·5	1·1	1·9
(d) Durables	32·7	8·9	7·5	2·5	0·1	0·2	0·2	2·6	1·5	0·2	0·3	1·3
(e) Other	112·7	76·2	65·9	20·5	1·3	2·9	1·5	13·9	14·8	2·7	8·3	10·2
3. Government consumption	51·3	34·7	30·0	9·5	0·4	1·2	0·5	6·4	5·8	1·6	4·5	4·7
(a) General administration	11·1	18·6	15·3	3·5	0·2	0·7	0·3	4·0	3·0	0·8	2·9	3·3
(b) Defence	40·2	16·2	14·7	6·0	0·2	0·6	0·2	2·4	2·9	0·8	1·6	1·5
4. Domestic investment	74·4	53·0	45·9	10·7	1·1	2·5	0·9	13·7	8·3	2·5	6·2	7·1
(a) Producers' durables	30·1	21·4	19·2	5·1	0·4	1·4	0·5	5·2	3·7	1·2	1·8	2·3
(b) Construction	38·2	27·8	23·3	4·7	0·7	0·9	0·4	7·1	4·2	1·1	4·1	4·5
(i) Residential	12·8	15·5	13·4	2·9	0·3	0·6	0·2	5·3	2·1	0·4	1·6	2·1
(ii) Other	25·4	12·3	9·9	1·8	0·4	0·4	0·2	1·8	2·2	0·7	2·5	2·4
(c) Increase in stocks	6·1	3·8	3·5	0·9	0·0	0·2	0·0	1·4	0·4	0·2	0·4	0·3
5. Net exports	1·2	1·4	1·9	0·1	-0·1	0·3	0·0	0·9	0·7	0·2	-0·2	-0·5
6. Population	164·5	284·1	219·4	51·0	3·4	8·9	4·4	49·9	43·3	10·7	47·8	64·7

* Components do not always add up to totals because of rounding-off errors.

Germany and $659 in Italy; the amount of dollars per head spent on food in these same countries was respectively 382, 286, 287 and 195; that spent on consumers' durables, 198, 49, 52 and 6; that spent on fixed investment, 415, 192, 246 and 121; and that spent on public administration alone, 68, 69, 80 and 61. This last, exceptionally constant, series is a striking confirmation of the view that public administration is an overhead which varies directly with the number of inhabitants, irrespective of their average income.

In the third place, by dividing the items in each column by their sum (row 1) we can find out in what proportion each component of product contributes to the total. Taking the main categories first, we see that on the average private consumption accounts for about two-thirds of final product, public consumption for about one-seventh and fixed investment for about one-sixth, the remainder being made up of investment in stocks and net exports, both comparatively unimportant quantities. From country to country there are considerable variations from these averages, however, but they seem to be a matter of national idiosyncrasies, quite unconnected with either size or standard of living. For instance, in America and Italy, which are at the opposite ends of the income scale, the proportion of product devoted to consumption was the same, between 66 and 67 per cent, while in Denmark and the Netherlands, which are both in the middle range, it was 71 and 61 per cent respectively. The percentage devoted to public consumption ranged from 14 in America, Britain, the Netherlands and Italy to 10 in Denmark and only 9 in Norway. Fixed investment shows the same unpredictable pattern: in Britain the percentage was as low as 15, in Norway, with almost the same product per head, it was as high as 26.

We can get a more enlightening picture of the spending patterns of the different countries if we subdivide the main percentages into their subcomponents. All sorts of combinations and permutations are possible and the reader should have no difficulty in constructing his own tables of percentages in any way he thinks interesting. A summary which throws some light on the relationship between spending patterns and income levels is given in table 18 below as an example, with the European countries collected together in two groups: the first, called Northern and Western Europe, contains the richest seven of the eight; the second, called Southern Europe, is made up of Italy and the 'other' O.E.E.C. countries.

TABLE 18

The Allocation of Gross National Product in Relation to Product per Head in 1955

(Percentages and 1955 $)

	United States	Northern and Western Europe	Southern Europe
1. Percentages of gross national product*			
(a) Private consumption	66	67	69
(i) Food	17	24	29
(ii) Clothing	7	6	7
(iii) Housing	4	5	4
(iv) Consumers' durables	9	4	2
(v) Other goods and services	30	28	26
(b) Government consumption	14	12	13
(i) General administration	3	6	9
(ii) Defence	11	6	4
(c) Gross investment in fixed assets	18	18	18
(i) Producers' durables	8	9	6
(ii) Construction	10	9	12
(d) Increase in stocks and net exports ...	2	3	0
2. Gross national product per head (*in 1955* $) ...	2,293	1,189	623

* Percentages do not aways add up to totals because of rounding-off errors.

Bearing in mind that rich regions have more of all the main categories of goods and services than poor regions have, the conclusions to be drawn from this table are: (i) the richer the country the smaller the proportion of income spent on food and the larger the proportions spent on durables and other services, while those spent on clothing and housing stay constant; (ii) the poorer the country the larger the proportion of its resources absorbed by public administration and the smaller, as a general rule, that absorbed by defence; and

(iii) though in fixed investment the pattern is not so definite, it appears that the richer countries invest relatively more in producers' durables and relatively less in construction than do the poorer countries.

CHAPTER V

WHERE DO WE GO FROM HERE?

1. *Summary*

IN THE preceding chapters we have described the main conceptual problems which arise in accounting for the transactions in an economic system. We have shown how the main totals of income and product are related to one another and how they are built up from their constituents. We have discussed the question of comparing product totals over time and space and have explained how in making comparisons we must distinguish between figures expressed in the currency units of a particular place and time and those expressed in a common unit of purchasing power.

By these means we have introduced step by step the basic information needed to describe and compare economic systems in quantitative terms. This information has been organized within an accounting framework designed to distinguish between the activities of production, consumption and accumulation and between the domestic economy and the rest of the world. Before finally closing down we shall indicate briefly how by extending this framework we can increase the scope of our analysis and unite the main branches of economic statistics into a coherent system.

2. *Input-output*

When we were examining the domestic product account in section 3 of Chapter II above we imagined this account to have been constructed by consolidating all the production accounts in the economy. As a consequence we lost all the flows of intermediate product. If we want to study the productive system in detail we must retrieve this information, since in most industries a considerable part of the costs of production consists of purchases from other industries and in many industries a considerable part of the revenue from production comes from sales to other industries. We can do this by grouping the production accounts into classes so that we have one account for each branch of production. If we arrange these accounts in a system of rows and columns so that the elements in a given row relate to the revenues (outputs) of a particular industry and the elements in the corresponding column relate to the costs (inputs) of the same industry, we obtain the familiar form of input-output table. In addition to the industry rows and columns, this table will contain an extra row and column whose elements will be respectively the primary inputs into the different branches of production and the final outputs emerging from them.

The construction of input-output tables was pioneered about a generation ago by Leontief and applied by him to the American economy in [16, 17]. A fairly detailed numerical example for Britain in 1954, compiled by the Board of Trade and the Central Statistical Office, is given in [32]. The way in which the input-output table fits into the social accounts and the problems of classification and arrangement to which its construction gives rise are outlined in [31]. A fuller treatment of taxonomic questions, and a guide to the analysis of productive systems in general, will be found in [28]. An excellent survey of these subjects was published in 1959 by Chenery and Clark [7]. Nowadays, when the use of input-output tables has spread almost everywhere, more and more thought is being given to the need for bringing such tables up to date and projecting them into the future; a method for doing this is discussed and illustrated numerically in [6].

3. *The Distribution of Incomes*

Just as the domestic product account can be subdivided, so can any other. We have already seen an example of this applied to consumption in the discussion on sectors in section 8 of

Chapter II above. In that case we set up separate accounts for the private and public sectors, which when consolidated gave the income and outlay of the whole economy. Evidently we could carry this process further; we could for instance set up within the private sector three separate income and outlay accounts, one for companies, one for non-profit-making institutions and one for individuals, and these in their turn could be further subdivided, according to size or type of income, geographical location, type of activity or any other classification we liked.

While the subdivision by size of income is not very significant in the case of companies and institutions, it is of considerable interest where individuals are concerned. In spite of this it is not usual to find complete accounts for individuals in different income groups, though there is no difficulty in finding particular items divided in this way. Thus table 21 of the *Blue Book* gives, for certain chosen years, quite detailed information on the distribution of income before and after tax; being based mainly on tax assessments, however, it inevitably leaves a certain amount of income unallocated, and its definitions are such that the figures cannot be interpreted without the help of [35, pp. 69–71]. Information on the distribution of incomes in America can be found in [48], [49] and [51, pp. 40–46].

Personal outlay, or at least the details of consumers' expenditure, can also be found distributed according to ranges of income in family-budget inquiries. A large investigation of this kind, carried out by the Ministry of Labour and National Service in connection with the revision of the index of retail prices, is described in [42]; and a continuing survey, carried out on a similar basis, appears periodically in [43]. It might be supposed that sample inquiries from households would provide the best basis for estimating and correctly allocating according to incomes the entries in the income and outlay accounts for individuals. In practice, however, it turns out that this approach is full of difficulties, as explained by Cole and Utting in [8] and other papers relating to the Cambridge Survey. More about the whole subject can be learnt from the results of the Oxford

Savings Survey as described for example by Lydall in [19].

For many purposes it is useful to have a mathematical expression for the distribution of incomes. From this we can obtain, among other things, a measure of concentration in terms of which we can say whether the incomes of one period or country are more or less concentrated than those of another period or country. The form of the distribution may be derived either from purely empirical considerations or from a model of the process of income formation. Much of the immense amount of work on this subject is conveniently summarized for mathematical readers by Aitchison and Brown in [1].

4. *The Flow of Funds and Moneyflows*

When we come to capital transactions we again find that on subdividing the national accounts by sectors we obtain a large number of flows which had been lost when the sector accounts were consolidated. For instance, by consolidation we had lost all the flows of funds whereby one sector puts its savings, either by means of loans or by means of transfers, at the disposal of another. Information of this kind is particularly desirable if we wish to study monetary phenomena, and from this point of view we should focus our attention on sectors which were hardly noticeable when studying production and consumption. For example, financial intermediaries such as banks, insurance companies, building societies and the like play an important role in the direction of funds although their role in production and consumption is of secondary importance.

Until fairly recently not much research had been done in Britain on this subject, but since the publication of the report of the Radcliffe Committee on the working of the monetary system [39] British financial statistics have been very considerably improved. From 1964 onwards a substantial amount of information on flows of funds has been published in the *Blue Book*. This work is discussed by Berman in [2]. A detailed study for 1963 is being undertaken as part of the Cambridge Growth Project [4, 5, 6].

For America, an accounting system intended to emphasize this aspect of economic transactions was first devised by Copeland in [9] as a study of 'moneyflows' and has been developed by the Federal Reserve System in [47]. Up-to-date information appears from time to time in [46].

5. *Regional Balances of Payments*

The account for the rest of the world in table 6 above was made up of all the loose ends from the three accounts for production, consumption and accumulation, and thus closed the system. The entries in this account were arranged in a particular way which was convenient for the purpose in hand. They could however be elaborated and rearranged to provide a detailed statement of incomings and outgoings between Britain and the rest of the world. Even so, in many cases a simple account treating the rest of the world as if it were a single entity is not enough; it is necessary to have an articulated set of accounts in which each type of transaction that the country has with the outside world will be subdivided and appropriately distributed among different economic regions. Detailed information on the British balance of payments, with some subdivision of the rest of the world into economic regions such as Western Europe and the overseas sterling area, is given in [38]; earlier estimates for the years 1946–57 were published in [41]. Similar information for America is to be found in [50]. A general survey of methods of regional description and analysis is contained in [29].

6. *National Balance Sheets*

All the concepts which have so far been described relate to *flows*, that is so much produced, consumed, due to be paid, due to be received, transferred, lent, borrowed, etc., *per unit of time*. To obtain a complete accounting system we must also account for *stocks*, not in the limited sense of products awaiting sale or use but in the more general sense of *assets* and *liabilities* existing *at a point in time*; that is to say, we must set up a national *balance sheet*. In a world in which values were constant this balance sheet might be presented in a form similar to the account for capital transactions, except that in front of each item we should have to put the word 'accumulated' to show that the figures referred to the total stock accumulated over the past and not to the latest addition to that stock represented by the flow for the current period; we should also omit the accumulated depreciation from liabilities and subtract it from the accumulated fixed investment which forms the major component of assets. A table thus drawn up would show on the assets side the wealth of the economy as composed of: (i) the depreciated (written-down) value of all fixed assets; (ii) the value of stocks in the narrow sense of raw materials not yet used up, goods for sale and work in progress; and (iii) net claims outstanding against the rest of the world. On the liabilities side the table would show the capital financing this wealth as composed of: (i) the accumulated saving of the economy; and (ii) the accumulated capital transfers (net) from the rest of the world. In practice, values do not remain constant and so these simple relationships are complicated in various ways. We shall not pursue these complications here.

The construction of national balance sheets is related to the older studies of the national capital in the same way as the construction of national accounts is related to the older studies of the national income; but work on stocks has lagged behind work on flows, and balance sheets have not yet become an integral part of the national accounts. In recent years, however, some progress has been made. An interesting study of the structure of property ownership in Britain in the mid-1950's was published by Morgan in [21]; and the first fruits of Revell's work at Cambridge on national and sector balance sheets in the years 1957–61 have now appeared in [26]. For America the outstanding work on this subject is that carried out by Goldsmith and has been published in a number of books and papers of which the latest are [13, 14].

7. *Social Accounting*

The term *social accounting*, as opposed to *national accounting*, is used to denote the activity of designing and constructing a system of accounts which will embrace all the ramifications of an economy, as far as these are measurable, and so will include all the extensions of the national accounts which have just been described. We entitled Chapter II 'From national income to national accounts', that is to say the transition from a *single magnitude*, the basic total of income, to a *structure* in which this magnitude is related to others of a similar kind. The transition from national accounts to social accounts involves perhaps a smaller step conceptually, the replacement of a simple structure by a more elaborate one rather than the replacement of a magnitude by a structure, but a much bigger step from a practical point of view, because the amount of additional data required for the second transition is very large and its integration into a coherent system presents formidable difficulties.

One problem which is central to the development of social accounting is the reconciliation of competing classifications which arise as various extensions of the national accounts are attempted. For example, in national accounting it is usual to give a classification of consumers' expenditure by commodities which follows roughly the lines of a shopping list; in input-output accounting, on the other hand, the classification is based on industries and this, while in theory similar to a classification by commodities, will in fact differ considerably from the shopping list. Are we to retain both these classifications, and if so how can we integrate them? A similar problem arises in fitting into a single system the production accounts in input-output and the capital transactions accounts dealing with flows of funds: in input-output the 'industries' are classified as producing units, in flow-of-funds they are classified as financing units. The two classifications are not the same and again the question arises: shall we be content with developing the two sets of accounts separately, bringing them together only in their consolidated form, or shall we try to show numerically just how the two 'industry' concepts are related? These and other such problems are discussed at length in [4, 5, 30], the second of which contains a fully elaborated social accounting matrix for Britain in 1960. This matrix is now being revised and similar matrices are being constructed for other years. In time, with the help of the work on flows of funds and on balance sheets mentioned in sections 4 and 6 above, there should emerge from this study a complete system of social accounts in which stocks are recorded as well as flows and the financial side of the economy is as adequately treated as the real side.

In a single country, let alone all over the world, it is almost inevitable that systems of national accounts and their extensions will start on different lines so that the resulting statistics will not be completely consistent. This is due largely to the insufficiency of the data but also partly to differences of purpose and partly to differences of approach to taxonomic problems. It is generally agreed that these differences lead to endless difficulties for the users of such investigations and that they should be avoided as far as possible. Much has been done by meetings and conferences to share experiences and to develop a common view on particular aspects of social accounting and explore the relationships between them. As already mentioned, the O.E.E.C. and the U.N. have set up standard systems of national accounts [23, 44] which by now are virtually the same, and have gone on to explore such problems as the construction of price and quantity index-numbers [27] and of input-output tables [28] within the framework of the social accounts. But an enormous amount remains still to be done.

8. *Social Accounting in Relation to Economic Theory and Analysis*

In conclusion we shall try to trace the connection between social accounting on the one hand and economic theory and analysis on the other. Social accounting is concerned with a comprehensive, orderly, consistent presentation of the facts of economic life, in which the concepts, definitions and classifications adopted lend themselves to actual measurement and, within this limitation, correspond to those which appear in economic theory and so can be used for economic analysis. Thus, even if we start from an empirical point of view we shall find ourselves listening to the suggestions of theory at every turn: it is not the facts themselves that lead us to distinguish between current and capital expenditure, we do so at the suggestion of theory despite the difficulties involved in carrying out the distinction; nor is it the facts themselves that lead us to emphasize the national income as the basic total both of a country's income and of its contribution to world production. And so it is all the way through. The facts we present and the way we arrange them depend a great deal on considerations of theory.

The same is true if we start from a theoretical point of view. We may begin with purely theoretical concepts, like utility, which we have not yet learnt how to measure, but somewhere along the line our theories must connect with concepts to which we can give an empirical content, and so enable us to state expectations about the real world. For if this link is missing we can hold any theory we wish provided it is logically consistent but we cannot speak of such a theory as being true or false since it says nothing about the real world and consequently cannot be supported or refuted by an appeal to facts. In other words, for a theory to be meaningful it must have empirical consequences and for it to be useful these consequences must relate to observable phenomena. Thus, useful theories cannot be developed independently of what can be observed any more than useful facts can be established without some regard to theoretical considerations.

Facts and theories meet in analysis. The combination of the two is essential if economics is to progress, since it is neither a pure subject, like mathematics, of which one does not ask that the theories should be applicable to actual phenomena, nor is it a collection of facts, like the objects on a junk heap, of which one does not ask how they are related. For 'balanced growth' in economics it is necessary to keep the facts and theories in line so that they can be related to one another. To help with this work is the main object of this book.

A LIST OF WORKS CITED

1. AITCHISON, J., and J. A. C. BROWN. *The Lognormal Distribution*. Cambridge University Press, 1957.
2. BERMAN, Lawrence. Flow of funds in the United Kingdom (with discussion). *Journal of the Royal Statistical Society, Series A*, vol. 128, pt. 3, 1965, pp. 321–60.
3. BOWLEY, Arthur L., and Josiah STAMP. *The National Income 1924*. Clarendon Press, Oxford, 1927.
4. CAMBRIDGE, DEPARTMENT OF APPLIED ECONOMICS. *A Computable Model of Economic Growth*. No. 1 in *A Programme for Growth*. Chapman and Hall, London, 1962.
5. CAMBRIDGE, DEPARTMENT OF APPLIED ECONOMICS. *A Social Accounting Matrix for 1960*. No. 2 in *A Programme for Growth*. Chapman and Hall, London, 1962.
6. CAMBRIDGE, DEPARTMENT OF APPLIED ECONOMICS. *Input-Output Relationships, 1954–1966*. No. 3 in *A Programme for Growth*. Chapman and Hall, London, 1963.
7. CHENERY, Hollis B., and Paul G. CLARK. *Interindustry Economics*. Wiley, New York, 1959.
8. COLE, Dorothy, and J. E. G. UTTING. Estimating expenditure, saving and income from household budgets (with discussion). *Journal of the Royal Statistical Society, Series A*, vol. 119, pt. 4, 1956, pp. 371–92.
9. COPELAND, Morris A. *A Study of Moneyflows in the United States*. National Bureau of Economic Research, New York, 1952.
10. FISHER, Irving. *The Making of Index Numbers*. Houghton Mifflin Co., Boston and New York, third edition, 1927.
11. GEARY, R. C. A note on the comparison of exchange rates and purchasing power between countries. *Journal of the Royal Statistical Society, Series A*, vol. 121, pt. 1, 1958, pp. 97–9.

12. GILBERT, Milton, and Associates. *Comparative National Products and Price Levels*. O.E.E.C., Paris, 1958.

13. GOLDSMITH, Raymond W. *The National Wealth of the United States in the Postwar Period*. Princeton University Press, Princeton, 1962.

14. GOLDSMITH, Raymond W., Robert E. LIPSEY and Morris MENDELSON. *Studies in the National Balance Sheet of the United States*. Two volumes. Princeton University Press, Princeton, 1963.

15. IJZEREN, J. van. Three methods of comparing the purchasing power of currencies. *Statistical Studies*, no. 7, December 1956. Uitgeversmaatschappij W. de Haan N.V., Zeist, 1957, for The Netherlands Central Bureau of Statistics.

16. LEONTIEF, Wassily W. Quantitative input and output relations in the economic system of the United States. *The Review of Economic Statistics*, vol. XVIII, no. 3, 1936, pp. 105–25.

17. LEONTIEF, Wassily W. *The Structure of American Economy*. 1st edition (*1919–1929*), Harvard University Press, Cambridge, Mass., 1941; 2nd edition (*1919–1939*), Oxford University Press, New York, 1951.

18. LOMAX, K. S. Production and productivity movements in the United Kingdom since 1900 (with discussion). *Journal of the Royal Statistical Society*, Series A, vol. 122, pt. 2, 1959, pp. 185–220.

19. LYDALL, H. F. *British Incomes and Savings*. Blackwell, Oxford, 1955.

20. MEADE, J. E., and Richard STONE. *National Income and Expenditure*. Bowes and Bowes, London, fourth edition, 1957.

21. MORGAN, E. Victor. *The Structure of Property Ownership in Great Britain*. Clarendon Press, Oxford, 1960.

22. O. E. C. D. *Seasonal Adjustment on Electronic Computers*. O.E.C.D., Paris, 1960.

23. O. E. E. C. *A Standardised System of National Accounts*. O.E.E.C., Paris, 1952; *1958 edition*, 1959.

24. PAIGE, Deborah, and Gottfried BOMBACH. *A Comparison of National Output and Productivity of the United Kingdom and the United States*. Joint study by O.E.E.C. and D.A.E., Cambridge. O.E.E.C., Paris, 1959.

25. REDDAWAY, W. B. (editor). *Key Statistics of the British Economy, 1900–1964*. London and Cambridge Economic Service. The Times Publishing Co., London, 1965.

26. REVELL, Jack. The wealth of the nation. *Moorgate and Wall Street*, spring, 1966.

27. STONE, Richard. *Quantity and Price Indexes in National Accounts*. O.E.E.C., Paris, 1956.

28. STONE, Richard. *Input-Output and National Accounts*. O.E.E.C., Paris, 1961.

29. STONE, Richard. Social accounts at the regional level: a survey. In *Regional Economic Planning*, O.E.E.C., Paris, 1961.

30. STONE, Richard. Multiple classifications in social accounting. *Bulletin of the International Statistical Institute*, vol. XXXIX, no. 3, 1962, pp. 215–33.

31. STONE, Richard, and Giovanna CROFT-MURRAY. *Social Accounting and Economic Models*. Bowes and Bowes, London, 1959.

32. U.K., BOARD OF TRADE and CENTRAL STATISTICAL OFFICE. *Input-Output Tables for the United Kingdom, 1954*. Studies in Official Statistics, no. 8. H.M.S.O., London, 1961.

33. U. K., CENTRAL STATISTICAL OFFICE. *Economic Trends*. H.M.S.O., London, monthly.

34. U. K., CENTRAL STATISTICAL OFFICE. *National Income and Expenditure*. H.M.S.O., London, annually.

35. U. K., CENTRAL STATISTICAL OFFICE. *National Income Statistics: Sources and Methods*. H.M.S.O., London, 1956.

36. U. K., CENTRAL STATISTICAL OFFICE. *Preliminary Estimates of National Income and Balance of Payments*. H.M.S.O., London, annually.

37. U. K., CENTRAL STATISTICAL OFFICE. *The Index of Industrial Production: Method of Compilation.* H.M.S.O., London, 1959.

38. U. K., CENTRAL STATISTICAL OFFICE. *United Kingdom Balance of Payments.* H.M.S.O., London, annually since 1963.

39. U. K., COMMITTEE ON THE WORKING OF THE MONETARY SYSTEM (Radcliffe Committee). *Report.* Cmnd. 827. H.M.S.O., London, 1959.

40. U. K., H.M. TREASURY. *Economic Report.* H.M.S.O., London, annually.

41. U. K., H.M. TREASURY. *United Kingdom Balance of Payments 1946–1957.* H.M.S.O., London, 1959.

42. U. K., MINISTRY OF LABOUR AND NATIONAL SERVICE. *Report of an Enquiry into Household Expenditure in 1953–54.* H.M.S.O., London, 1957.

43. U.K., MINISTRY OF LABOUR. *Family Expenditure Survey.* H.M.S.O., London, periodically.

44. U. N., STATISTICAL OFFICE. *A System of National Accounts and Supporting Tables.* U.N., New York, 1953; *Revision 1,* 1960.

45. U. N., STATISTICAL OFFICE. *Yearbook of National Accounts Statistics.* U.N., New York, annually since 1957.

46. U. S., BOARD OF GOVERNORS OF THE FEDERAL RESERVE SYSTEM. *Federal Reserve Bulletin.* Board of Governors of the Federal Reserve System, Washington, monthly.

47. U. S., BOARD OF GOVERNORS OF THE FEDERAL RESERVE SYSTEM. *Flow of Funds in the United States 1939–1953.* Board of Governors of the Federal Reserve System, Washington, 1955.

48. U. S., DEPARTMENT OF COMMERCE. *Income Distribution in the United States by Size, 1944–1950.* U.S. Government Printing Office, Washington, 1953.

49. U. S., DEPARTMENT OF COMMERCE. *Survey of Current Business.* U.S. Government Printing Office, Washington, monthly.

50. U. S., DEPARTMENT OF COMMERCE. *The Balance of Payments of the United States.* U.S. Government Printing Office, Washington, annually.

51. U. S., DEPARTMENT OF COMMERCE. *U.S. Income and Output.* A supplement to the *Survey of Current Business.* U.S. Government Printing Office, Washington, 1959.